D1196543

Kentucky Lawyer

Kentucky Lawyer

MAC SWINFORD

THE UNIVERSITY PRESS OF KENTUCKY

Scholarly publisher for the Commonwealth,
serving Bellarmine University, Berea College, Centre College of
Kentucky, Eastern Kentucky University, The Filson Historical Society,
Georgetown College, Kentucky Historical Society, Kentucky State
University, Morehead State University, Murray State University,
Northern Kentucky University, Transylvania University, University of
Kentucky, University of Louisville, and Western Kentucky University.
All rights reserved.

Editorial and Sales Offices: The University Press of Kentucky
663 South Limestone Street, Lexington, Kentucky 40508-4008
www.kentuckypress.com

Frontispiece: Mac Swinford as a guest during the first broadcast of
Comment on Kentucky, November 11, 1974.

12 11 10 09 08   5 4 3 2 1

Library of Congress Cataloging-in-Publication Data

Swinford, Mac.
  Kentucky lawyer / Mac Swinford.
    p. cm.
  Rev. ed. of: Cincinnati : W.H. Anderson Co., [1963]
  ISBN 978-0-8131-2480-3 (hardcover : alk. paper)
  1. Judges—Kentucky—Biography. 2. Lawyers—Kentucky. I. Title.
  KF373.S94A3 2008
  340.092—dc22
  [B]   2007044806

This book is printed on acid-free recycled paper meeting
the requirements of the American National Standard
for Permanence in Paper for Printed Library Materials.

Manufactured in the United States of America.

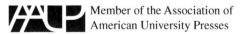 Member of the Association of
American University Presses

I dedicate this small volume
to the one who represented to me
the finest traditions of the bar of Kentucky
for seventy-three years,
my father, M. C. Swinford,
lawyer, gentleman.

Contents

Foreword

I first met Judge Mac Swinford when he and Judge Bernard T. Moynahan Jr. administered my oath of office as U.S. attorney for the Eastern District of Kentucky in January 1970. Of course, like all lawyers in Kentucky, I had heard many legends about Judge Swinford. The more I was around him, the more I admired him as a judge and as a person.

Judge Swinford and I had similar backgrounds, although he was a Presbyterian Democrat and I was a Baptist Republican. We both came from small towns where our families had lived in our respective counties for many years. We both attended the University of Virginia law school, and I still have his old framed photograph of the university, taken about the time he attended school there.

Judge Swinford had also served as the U.S. attorney for the Eastern District of Kentucky. President Franklin D. Roosevelt appointed him when Judge Swinford was only thirty-three. When Congress authorized an additional judgeship for both federal districts in Kentucky, Judge Swinford was appointed to the district court by President Roosevelt in 1937, when he was thirty-seven.

I strove to model my judicial career after that of Judge

Swinford. He was always patient and believed in the dignity of every human being. Even when he was strict in sentencing offenders, he addressed them personally and tried to encourage them to lead fruitful lives upon their release from incarceration.

During the years when I knew him, Judge Swinford had a full head of silver hair and his authoritative manner gave lawyers and litigants alike the feeling that they were in the presence of God or one of His appointed angels. Attorneys in his court were fond of appearing before him, and I never heard any lawyer speak ill of him.

He was the only judge I ever knew who gave instructions to the jury off the top of his head. Over the many years he served on the bench, he memorized the instructions, so he would look the jury straight in the eye and recite to them the instructions for the case. All he used was an outline on a yellow pad that he had written out as the trial progressed. Rarely did either side in a criminal case need to request additional instructions from Judge Swinford, for he covered every relevant aspect of the trial in his instructions.

Although he was not from the mountains, Judge Swinford told me that he always enjoyed presiding in court in London, Jackson, Pikeville and Catlettsburg. In the early years, he traveled to many of those locations by train. By virtue of his commission, he also presided over trials in the Western District of Kentucky, primarily in Bowling Green. Through his many experiences as a small-town lawyer, as a state legislator, as a U.S. attorney, and as a district judge, he picked up the wonderful stories that are included in his book. Lawyers for years recited many of these tales and lamented that copies of the book were impossible to find.

Everyone who knew Mac Swinford personally came to love and respect him. This printing of *Kentucky Lawyer* will enable those who did not know him to become acquainted with him.

It is an honor for me to have known him and all of his family.

Eugene E. Siler Jr.
Judge, U.S. Court of Appeals for the Sixth Circuit

Preface

Most of these stories have been taken from instances which I have personally witnessed or which have been related to me by first- or second-hand observers. I have scrupulously attempted to avoid offending any living person or the family or friends of those who are dead, and I have occasionally used fictitious names. The quotes are used liberally and not literally. Memory is frail. Language and conduct attributed to actors in past drama must be accepted in the complimentary spirit in which it is offered.

Mac Swinford
May 1963

Introduction

Someone has well said that the memory of its great men is a nation's most cherished inheritance. The term "great" is not always properly used. Greatness is a relative thing, and when speaking of great men we are inclined to think only of public men who hold high office and who are immortalized in history books as national or state political leaders, or men of science or achievement in some field of endeavor that is mentioned in the press or periodicals of the day. But all too frequently true greatness goes unnoticed and unrecorded.

American culture in its most intimate and significant sense is composed of the acts and expressions of local leaders in the everyday affairs of life. It is from these inconspicuous individuals that our nation derives much of its strength. They are the people who day after day in the little places of America meet the complexities of everyday life and the unglamorous business of just getting along, but in so doing preserve and strengthen the sinews of our democracy.

It is with a hope of preserving a part of this delightful fineness of our traditional Americanism that I write about the Kentucky lawyer and pay tribute to a group of men whom I have known and admired extremely.

When one undertakes to record some of his observations and experiences, he runs the risk of being accused of vanity; I hope that I shall not be so charged in this effort. The privilege of having the opportunity to observe at first hand these colorful and gifted men seems to place upon me an obligation to see to it that some of their contributions to our society, which might otherwise be lost to professional lore, are preserved. Do not understand me to say that the Kentucky lawyer or the members of the profession generally have been neglected by authors and historians. They have not. The guidance of lawyers to our government in its formation and preservation has received a full share of acknowledgment. Kentuckians especially have been well recognized in this respect. One cannot read American history without noting the important parts played by Henry Clay, John J. Crittenden, John G. Carlisle, John C. Breckinridge and numerous others, to say nothing of such men of national and world stature as Abraham Lincoln, Jefferson Davis, Alben W. Barkley, Supreme Court Justices John M. Harlan and Stanley F. Reed, and Chief Justice of the United States, Fred M. Vinson.

My concern in this book is primarily with the many lawyers in Kentucky who were and are capable of discharging a trust with honor and ability equal to that of the men mentioned above, but who, because of circumstance or purpose, have never become known beyond a local or statewide orbit.

No comment

In referring to Kentuckians, Harlan, Vinson and Reed, who became members of the Supreme Court of the United States, I am reminded of a very fine statement I heard Judge Alex P. Humphrey of Louisville make many years ago. I had just been admitted to the bar and the Kentucky State Bar Association was having its annual meeting at Estill Springs near Irvine. That was in the days of the old voluntary association and long before the integrated bar. I would not want to supplant the present system, but the old voluntary bar association is a pleasant memory. There were rarely over two hundred in attendance, and because of this small number the meetings could be held in small places.

Estill Springs was a charming place. The old frame hotel with its shrub-lined brick walk leading to the mineral spring from the wide veranda amid beautiful forest trees, perennial flowers and blooming vines, was a hostelry with much of the tradition of the old South. The interior was gracious and comfortable; its spaciousness in no way destroyed the atmosphere of congeniality. The food was abundant and delicious.

The smallness of the crowd made it easy to get acquainted with everyone. It was an education for a young lawyer to be in the company of and feel the warmth of friendship from older and eminent members of the bar. I had gone to the meeting with my father and mother, and one morning we were having breakfast with Judge Humphrey, who was considered the most distinguished member of the Kentucky bar. He was in his late seventies, but was still vigorous in mind and body. Like most truly great men he was kindly in manner and appeared to be much interested in me and what I thought of my prospects at the bar.

During the course of the meal my father said, "Judge Humphrey, is it true that you were once offered an appointment to the Supreme Court of the United States?" I shall never forget the reply of this perfect gentleman:

"Mr. Swinford," he said, "I appreciate the compliment in your question, but I have always heard that when a young man asks a young lady to marry him, she should either accept his proposal or never tell that it was made."

Voices in the night

The Estill Springs meeting calls to mind another incident that occurred there, but which I did not hear about until some years later from Mr. John P. McCartny of Flemingsburg. Mr. McCartny was a very able lawyer; his home and main offices were in Flemingsburg, but he had partners or associates in Carlisle and Mt. Olivet. He also practiced extensively in Mason, Bracken and Bourbon Counties. He was of medium height, of slender build, and never showed the slightest trace of vexation—even when things were going against him in hearings on motions or in the trial of a case.

County courthouses in the days before television, radio and all-day movies were the places where citizens looked for drama and excitement. It was about the only place, except church, where people in a country town could go for pleasure and enlightenment. When a term of court was in progress, the courtroom was usually well filled with spectators. Lawyers were watched with interest, and their names, for a time at least, became household words in the community. Their reputations were made by the way in which they conducted themselves in the courtroom.

Mr. McCartny's courtly manner and temperament fitted right into this type of advertising. While not intentionally "playing to the stands," he must, nevertheless, have been at all times mindful of the presence of an audience. He would argue his points on demurrers and motions vigorously. If his position was sustained, he bowed to the court and thanked the judge for his ruling. If he was overruled, he bowed and thanked the court with equal graciousness, and smilingly took his seat. To the lay onlookers, who neither clearly heard nor understood the legal technicalities and language used, he was successful even when unsuccessful. They would nudge and nod to each other and impliedly say, "Well, John's won again." They would leave the courtroom definitely convinced that if they or their families or friends ever needed a lawyer, John P. McCartny of Flemingsburg would be the best they could find. They had watched him in court for an entire day and he had never lost a single point.

But let us get back to the bar meeting at Estill Springs. Mr. McCartny said that he had arrived at the hotel early in the afternoon before the meeting, which was scheduled to begin on the following morning. He was shown to the room for which he had made a reservation many days in advance. It was an attractive and comfortable room with a double bed. Having settled himself in his room, he went to dinner and was soon having a most pleasant time, renewing old acquaintances and friendships as the other lawyers arrived.

At ten o'clock he retired to his room, for he was a man of regular habits and no vices, and he wanted to get a good night's rest in anticipation of the morrow and an interesting program. He had hardly gotten to sleep when he was awakened by a noise outside his door—a knock and someone calling his name:

"John, wake up and let me in!"

He went to the door and found that he had been awakened by the voice and knock of Judge Richard P. Stoll of Lexington. Judge Stoll, one of the most delightful and personable men at the bar and one of the best judges who ever sat on a Kentucky bench, had been enjoying the fellowship of congenial friends and convivial entertainment. To say that he was slightly under the weather would have been something of an understatement. The Judge explained that he had failed to make a reservation and had no place to sleep. He was of course cordially welcomed to share Mr. McCartny's double bed for the remainder of the night.

Judge Stoll was a man of very robust build. He had been a famous football player at the University of Kentucky and the years (he was at that time about fifty-five) had added considerable flesh to his muscular body; he weighed in the vicinity of two hundred and thirty pounds.

Nevertheless, McCartny managed to get Judge Stoll into the room where he proceeded to assist him to undress and get into bed. This was something of an ordeal, but when it was finally accomplished, McCartny got into bed himself and attempted to go back to sleep. However, he was hardly as comfortable as he might have been, since the sprawling hulk of his bedfellow was taking up most of the space; indeed, there was only a small margin of mattress left to him. Notwithstanding this discomfort, the weariness of a day's travel and numerous handshakes and greetings of friends since his arrival at the springs overtook him, and he fell asleep.

At some later hour he was aroused by a chorus outside his window singing "Sweet Adeline" and "Down by the Old Mill Stream." Shortly thereafter a loud knock came on the door and upon opening it he saw standing before him one of the revelers, somewhat disheveled and obviously ready for bed. This gentleman was truly a "mister five by five"—the Honorable Presley Kimball of the Lexington bar, advocate of renown and orator of the old school. The knock on the door and the commotion of opening it aroused Dick Stoll, who jumped from the bed and welcomed the new arrival with open arms, inviting him to come in and spend the night. Unsteadily Pres entered the room and hastily accepted the invitation; he also was without reservations at the hotel.

To an ordinary man this double intrusion would have been irritating, but not the suave and kindly McCartny. He, too, invited Mr. Kimball to occupy the bed, fully realizing that he himself would have to find other quarters. The next problem was to get Pres undressed. As has been pointed out, Mr. Kimball was a short fat man, and at that moment was in a state of well-being that made him willing to accept without objection all valet service. Stoll succeeded in getting his coat off while Mr. McCartny untied and removed his shoes and trousers. The shirt posed a greater problem, for in those days men's shirts were of a different design from those of today: they did not button all the way down the front so as to be put on and off like a coat; instead they had a gusset effect of buttoning down about half way, thus making it necessary to put them on and off over the head.

At this point it is necessary to digress momentarily from our story and make known the fact that John McCartny and Dick Stoll were ardent Republicans and had been more or less active in party politics for a good many years. Kimball was an unreconstructed Rebel Democrat.

When the time came to remove Mr. Kimball's shirt, the undressers got the garment only half off and were unable then to pull it completely over the rotund little man's head; nor were they able to get it back on his plump body for a fresh start. They worked diligently with, of course, no help from the wearer of the shirt. The result was that Kimball was now effectively in a strait jacket. It was at this stage that Pres found his voice and began to yell with a great deal of gusto as well as volume:

"Help! Help! I've fallen into the hands of the Republicans! I've fallen into the hands of the Republicans!"

His shouts roused the entire hotel, and lawyers of both political parties sprang from their beds and rushed to the aid of their terrified brother barrister. Eventually the tumult subsided and tranquility was restored to the point that the shirt could be removed over the captive's head. Dick and Pres were carefully tucked into bed by McCartny who fortunately was able to find a cot in the kitchen; there he spent the remainder of the night in restful sleep.

Attributes of the Kentucky lawyer

Kentucky may be said to be divided into five main regions: the Mountains, the Blue Grass, the Bear Grass, the "Pennyrile," and the Purchase. There are, of course, colloquialisms in these respective sections which might be said to be marks of identification; but the line of demarcation is so fine that it hardly warrants comment. My years of travel in all parts of the state in conducting the business of the federal courts have given me an opportunity to become acquainted with Kentucky lawyers at first hand. I have had probably a better opportunity to know and observe them than most any other person. There are excellent lawyers, good lawyers, mediocre and poor lawyers in all of the regions; but there are two outstanding characteristics which belong to all the lawyers of the state: Kentucky lawyers are, as a class, men of honor and integrity; they are also very resourceful.

In my years on the bench I have never once had a show of discourtesy or disrespect. I fully realize that this is not because of me personally but because of the high office which I am privileged to hold. The office receives this respect, and justly so, because of the character and ability of the men who have preceded me in the office. It is due to them and their learning, erudition and fairness, that the bar accepts me on the terms which my predecessors have established. I am constantly aware of this, and my only fear is that in some careless moment I may say or do something, either on or off the bench, that could bring the slightest disrespect to the office which has stood so high in Kentucky jurisprudence for so long

All too frequently judges, in the security of their position, forget the problems and deep emotions of the attorneys who are practicing before them. There have been instances, I know, in which the judge seems to feel that the bench is a stage from which he, as chief actor in the drama of the trial, must perform as a wit or a tyrant. There have been judges who have become obsessed with a desire to be "characters" and have indulged in witticisms or abuses that are fitting neither the dignity of the office nor the stature of the personality that temporarily occupies it.

The story is told of an occasion in the trial of an important lawsuit when the judge in a fit of anger, sharply and without excuse, severely rebuked one of the attorneys. The lawyer then turned his back on the court and walked toward the door of the courtroom. The judge called out, "Sir, are you trying to show your contempt for the court?"

"No, Your Honor, I'm trying to conceal it," was the reply.

An "overspeaking" judge

Sir Francis Bacon in his essay on the judiciary said: "An overspeaking judge is no well-tuned cymbal." Those of our profession who occupy the bench should be constantly aware of this striking metaphor. It is very tempting at times for a judge to make witty or sarcastic remarks to the delight of the spectators; however, a judge should always remember that such speech is beneath the dignity of the court and always at the expense of someone who cannot answer back. The situation is something like that of a boxer who hits a handcuffed opponent. Repartee can be delightful and stimulating when the participants are on a common footing, but it is contemptible when one of them must yield to authority.

I have tried always to avoid this sort of thing; however, on one occasion at Bowling Green, I fell into it. Judge Robert M. Coleman, one of the best lawyers in Western Kentucky and a highly ethical practitioner, was making his final argument in a case that had extended over eight days. Judge Coleman had been speaking about thirty minutes of the forty-five minutes allotted him. He remarked to the jury that he knew they were tired and he wasn't going to prolong his argument. He then turned to the bench and asked, "Judge, how long have I been talking?"

"Too long," I replied without thinking. This remark from the bench got a laugh from the audience and I expect agreement from the jurors, but it was inexcusable in me and I felt embarrassed at the slip. I immediately apologized to Judge Coleman and assured the jury that my remark was not only inappropriate but untrue as well, for the gentleman still had fifteen minutes in which to conclude his speech.

According to law or instructions

While, generally speaking, judges are shielded from the real sentiments of those before them in the courtroom, there are occasions when the truth comes from the naive. A friend of mine serving on the federal bench in a neighboring state has told me of an experience he had with a juror. At the conclusion of the evidence and arguments he had charged the jury on the law of the case and sent it to the jury room for its deliberations. About half an hour later the marshal appeared and advised the judge that the jury wanted to see him in the jury room.

"I can't go up there, but you may bring them down and I'll see what they want," replied the judge.

When the jury appeared in the courtroom, the judge inquired, "Gentlemen, what seems to be your trouble; is it one of law or fact?"

The foreman replied, "Your Honor, the jury is divided. Some of them want to decide the case according to law, and some of them want to decide it according to your instructions."

At this innocent remark the mirth from the attorneys in the court could hardly be concealed. The judge's irritation was apparent; he rapped on the bench with his gavel and said, "Here, sir, you cannot talk like that to this court; I'll hold you in contempt of court."

"No, no, Judge," the frightened foreman replied, "you shouldn't hold me in contempt of court. I don't want to decide the case according to law; I'm one of those that want to decide it according to your instructions."

Namesake

While he was not a Kentuckian by birth but a native of our sister state of Tennessee, Judge George Taylor of Knoxville was a kindred spirit with Kentuckians in his fine sense of humor and ability to see the ridiculous side of courtroom instances, even when they involved himself. He told of an occasion at Greenville when a woman was before him with a plea of guilty for operating a moonshine still. Judge Taylor examined the probation officer's report and saw that the defendant was the mother of ten children. He looked up at her standing quietly as she awaited her sentence.

"I see," said the judge, "that you are the mother of ten children."

"Yes, sir," she meekly replied.

"I also notice," continued Judge Taylor, "that your last child was born after this indictment was returned. Is that true?"

With a bright smile on her face she responded hopefully, "Yes, sir, Judge, and I named him for you."

Sturdy oak

While it may be said that some judges affect a false air of importance and endeavor to establish themselves as legendary figures, there are others whose very presence and natural demeanor impress those with whom they come in contact, both on and off the bench, with their dignity and professional erudition. Such a one was the Honorable A. M. J. Cochran of Maysville, United States District Judge for the Eastern District of Kentucky, from the time of its establishment at the turn of the twentieth century until his death in 1934.

Judge Cochran was a graduate of Centre College and Harvard Law School. He was a man of wealth and aristocratic background, deeply learned both in liberal arts and the law. Notwithstanding his social prominence and independent wealth, he was of simple taste and a constant and indefatigable worker. In his thirty-three years on the bench, he never took a vacation and never left the state of Kentucky except on one occasion. At that time he went to Washington, D.C., to appear before a congressional committee to oppose, which he did successfully, the division of his district and the establishment of a third federal judicial district in Kentucky.

In appearance Judge Cochran was most distinctive: he was tall, spare, and had shaggy sideburns that came down on his cheeks to his lower jaw; on his thin face these sideburns gave him a very austere look indeed. He wore, in both winter and summer, black suits of the finest broadcloth and silk.

He was rarely seen in company with others and usually while attending court ate alone and spent his hours off the bench in his hotel room. Those of us who were privileged to know Judge Cochran intimately knew that beneath this somewhat forbidding exterior he was a man of deep sympathy and kindness, never unmindful of the feelings and rights of all who came before him, whether as litigants, witnesses or attorneys.

John W. Menzies of Covington probably knew the judge better than any other person outside his family. Clerk of the court for the Eastern District of Kentucky for many years and later clerk of the Court of Appeals for the Sixth Circuit at Cincinnati for another many years, Mr. Menzies, a most personable and charming gentleman and a storyteller of exception, could entertain by the hour with incidents of the courtroom while he served with Judge Cochran.

When I became United States Attorney I was thirty-three and the judge was near eighty. We were of different political faiths and possibly adhered to widely different economic principles, but we soon became warm friends. It was during prohibition and the criminal dockets were very heavy. There were numerous civil cases including two hundred and twelve war risk insurance cases in which the government was involved. I was before the court almost constantly. As I look back upon those hectic days, I realize how my inexperience must have been irritating to the court, but Judge Cochran always treated me with the greatest deference. If his patience was severely tested, he gave no evidence of it. I shall always cherish his memory for his consideration and kindness to me.

During my service as United States Attorney under Judge Cochran, a very amusing thing occurred one time at the regular term of court at London. We had an unusually heavy criminal docket, growing out of an intensive drive against persons using the mails to defraud by sending orders for goods in fictitious names, false letters of credit, and worthless checks. Complaints had come in from various mail-order houses, principally in Chicago and St. Louis. I had not directed an investigation at once as I knew the great expense to which the government would be put in order to complete an effective investigation and the difficulty there would be in getting the persons actually responsible for the acts. The fraudulent practice had become so widespread and persistent, however, that I had asked the postoffice department to provide a sufficient number of trained inspectors to go into Clay, Laurel, and other counties in that locality where the offenders were currently most numerous, and make a thorough study of the situation.

I had talked with the inspectors before they had gone and had told them not to arrest anybody who for any reason "couldn't go to jail." This phrase may need an explanation. I knew that among those who were defrauding the mail-order houses there were more women than men because the orders were principally for women's and children's clothing and costumes and because the women were in most cases more intelligent and better educated and could write more legibly; moreover, I was fully aware that both the court and I would be bound to recognize the two almost ironclad excuses for probation: pregnancy of at least six months duration and nursing a baby. I have never felt that one should have to start life from a jail maternity ward nor that a nursing baby should have to be weaned or sent to jail because of its mother's misdoings.

Probated sentences were not effective in this character of offense and would not break up the practice of using the mails to defraud the mail-order houses. So therefore, I wanted offenders to be left without arrest or to be of such qualifications that there would be no doubt of their guilt and no excuses or appendages to keep them from serving a sentence; for I proposed to recommend that they be sent to jail for short periods of time.

The investigation had extended over two months and one hundred and thirty-five persons had been placed under arrest. There was a singular thing about this matter which I feel is worth mentioning. I had instructed the inspectors not to take any of those placed under arrest into custody but merely to tell them they were under arrest as violators of the federal postal laws and must appear at the London Federal Building on a certain date which was the first day of court, and to exact a definite promise from each of them that he or she would obey the directive.

Here is a study for psychologists. Of the one hundred thirty-five people who had been lying and cheating through the mails, one hundred thirty-four of them kept their word and appeared at the appointed time. The single exception was two hours late and explained his tardiness, truthfully, I am sure, by stating that he had missed connections for a ride and had had to walk nine and a half miles.

But to get back to the incident of the appearance of these offenders, they were indicted and all called before the court for their pleas. All promptly plead guilty and, on my recommendation, Judge Cochran sentenced them to from thirty to ninety days in jail. They were so poor, a fine meant nothing; so none was imposed. Along about the middle of the call of the docket, a woman appeared before the court gaudily dressed in her recently purchased finery; she was carrying and eight- or nine-months-old baby.

Strange to say, nearly all of the defendants wore the clothes that had been sent from the mail-order houses on the fraudulent orders. I suppose they thought this was their big day and they had to dress up. The woman with the baby plead guilty but told a pathetic tale of how she would have to leave the child and her five other small children with strangers if she were required to go to jail. I was impressed and I think the judge was too. While it looked hardly fair to the other defendants to make an exception, recalling Emerson's words that "consistency is the hobgoblin of little minds," I recommended probation, which was granted.

Two or three more defendants appeared and were sentenced, then another woman appeared with a child. Forgetting Emerson this time and recalling, "O, consistency, thou art a jewel," I recommended that this defendant's sentence be probated in view of the probation of the other woman with the child. The court so ruled. The next woman defendant who appeared carried a child, and the next, and the next. All of them received probation.

I began to feel a little disheartened that my carefully laid plans to stop the mail fraud racket were falling through. The clerk called the next case; this one, too, was a woman with a child. But this time things were different; the child was crying and trying to fight the woman away from him. She was seeking to comfort him as she came down the aisle to the bench. I became suspicious and on closer inspection was convinced that the child had been there before—and on more than one occasion that day. I went to the bench and whispered my suspicious to the court.

The judge leaned over the bench and said, "Madam, is that your child?"

"No, Judge," she answered.

Judge Cochran became incensed at this effort of deception. "Then what are you doing with it?" he almost shouted.

"Judge," she said, somewhat frightened, "a lady in the hall just asked me to hold it for her." Needless to say, she got no probated sentence. We like for our children to have wholesome experiences, but being held by a defendant while she goes into court and pleads guilty to a felony is the type of experience children can do without.

An investigation disclosed that when the first woman succeeded in getting placed on probation because of her child, the air among the waiting defendants became electrified with new hope. The trouble was that there was only one baby in the crowd. However, the mother was not only a good advocate for her cause, she was an enterprising business woman as well. Seeing a chance to make a fast dime, she had stood at the door and rented the baby for ten cents to each defendant willing to pay. Some of the women were relatives and neighbors whom the baby knew, but the last woman was a total stranger, and becoming frightened, he refused to cooperate.

"Less sympathy—more consideration"

Another of the interesting stories concerning Judge Cochran occurred during World War I while he was holding court at Covington. The times required certain emergency legislation, presumably to protect the men in the armed forces from vice and its consequences. There was an act of Congress which made it a misdemeanor to run a house of prostitution within three miles of an army post. A notorious madam by the name of Alice Karris of Newport either had not heard of the law or had decided to presume upon the laxness of war times; and with an eye to business she continued to conduct this most ancient of professions. Her place was within the limits of Fort Thomas, and she was eventually brought before the federal court at Covington to answer an indictment charging a violation of the statute.

Alice Karris appeared in all her gaudy dress and professional air before Judge Cochran, who read to her the charge. She promptly pleaded guilty. We can picture this court scene with some degree of appreciation: a woman well into her seventies with all the marks of a misspent life. She was lavishly painted, and her hair was dyed a bright red, as, with an attempted air of pious martyrdom, she stood before the dignified elderly judge.

Before entering sentence, Judge Cochran delivered a moving patriotic address in which he referred to the fact that "our boys" were away from home, enlisted in a great cause of humanity—away from the care and protection of their mothers and fathers. He emphasized the importance of support of our government on the home front and pointed out that older people like the defendant and himself must be mindful of a high obligation of citizenship and duty and, although unable to bear arms, should, in their humble way, protect and defend our country and flag.

Obviously the audience in the courtroom was inspired to deep patriotic sentiment by the sight and eloquence of the tall, spare, distinguished aristocrat delivering a timely philippic to the aged and tearful Jezebel of the underworld who stood before him nodding her head and wiping her eyes with her soiled handkerchief. Judge Cochran was evidently impressed with his own words, for suddenly tears began to flow from his eyes. With this the culprit began to look more hopeful until she received the shock of the sentence—the maximum—five hundred dollars fine and six months in jail. Her remorseful countenance changed at once.

"Do you have anything to say?" the judge asked.

"Yes, sir, Judge, I do," came the prompt reply. "I'd rather you'd show me less sympathy and more consideration."

* * *

Speaking of sentences, I am reminded of an incident I overheard in court when I was a practicing attorney in Cynthiana. One of the prisoners who had been convicted a few days before was called before the bench and sentenced to life imprisonment with, as I now recall, the solemn words of the judge, "You are now hereby sentenced to the Kentucky State Penitentiary for the remainder of your natural life."

The prisoner was returned to the dock with the other prisoners who had also just received sentences for less serious offenses. The judge turned to the other business of the court, calling up motions in civil cases and hearing arguments.

I was sitting within earshot of the waiting prisoners, and after about an hour of the motion hearings I heard the man who had received the life sentence turn to the one near him and say in a stage whisper, "I wish this old guy would let us go back to jail. I want to start getting this sentence behind me."

Helping the judge

Another interesting incident in the judicial career of Judge Cochran occurred at Catlettsburg Court. Two attorneys were arguing very strenuously over a demurrer to the petition (motion to dismiss the complaint). The judge, apparently impressed with the position of the movant, was asking the plaintiff's attorney pointed questions that he was finding it difficult to answer and was presenting reasons which were giving the draftsman of the pleading obvious discomfort in anticipation of having his case dismissed. Not satisfied, however, with the way things were going, the attorney, on whose side of the question the judge was leaning, kept interrupting and putting in his own reasons and points. Finally, after numerous interruptions, Judge Cochran turned to the attorney and said, "Well, what's the matter, ain't I holding my own with him?"

This should be a lesson to the attorney who is guilty of such shortsightedness. All of us on the bench are familiar with him. Frequently, not satisfied with the points the court is making, he wants to insist on his particular views. When a judge appears to be taking an attorney's side of a proposition, that is a good time to keep quiet. If he decides for you, pick up your papers, leave the courthouse and go back to your office; prepare the order and present it for entry without delay. The court might change its mind.

"Pass the sugar"

One of the most colorful and brilliant characters ever at the Kentucky bar was the late Judge Edward C. O'Rear of Mt. Sterling and Frankfort. His career reads like a storybook, and he became, while yet living and actually practicing law, a legend of our profession and of our state. I recently heard that the combined lives of Judge O'Rear and his father covered a part of the term of every President of the United States from the time of George Washington down to John F. Kennedy.

Judge O'Rear was born in Montgomery County near the village of Camargo. His formal education was limited to only a few years at a one-room school. Yet he was one of the best educated and most scholarly men who ever served in our profession, either in Kentucky or elsewhere. His bright mind, ambition to succeed and indefatigable energy soon won him local fame after his admission to the bar of Montgomery County. It was not long until he was recognized as an eloquent orator and gifted speaker in the trial of lawsuits before either the court or jury and at social functions or political rallies.

He became a member and later Chief Justice of the Kentucky Court of Appeals. He carried his industry and willingness to work with him to Frankfort, and devoted the same talents and energy to the study of records and the preparation of opinions that he had given to his private law practice. His terse, forceful opinions immediately attracted the attention of the bar throughout the state, and almost without his knowledge he became recognized as an authority on the law in its manifold phases.

Notwithstanding his success as an appellate judge, he was not satisfied to make the bench a career. He longed for the excitement of the active participation in courtroom battles and the sharp contest of wits called for in the trial of a lawsuit. Those in our profession know this is unequaled in it compensation to those who love to match their steel with some worthy antagonist. The judge gave this account of his return to private practice:

"While I was at my office in the Judges' Chambers one morning, I decided to resign from the Appellate Court and open an office in Frankfort for the general practice of law. Delay seemed unnecessary, so I therewith wrote on a pad, 'I hereby resign from the Kentucky Court of Appeals, effective immediately,' and took it into the Governor's office and laid it on his desk. I got my hat and went home.

"My wife was naturally surprised to see me appear at home at 10:00 a. m. I explained my presence and told her of my plan to resume the practice of law. She was somewhat hesitant and not without a show of skepticism asked how we were going to live while I was building a practice. I explained that I had thought that out too. We were to practice severe economy as a start. We had a few hundred dollars in the bank which would provide food for us and the children for a few weeks.

"We would discharge the cook and the man of all work. She would do the cooking and I would do the chores, gardening, and such things as needed attention around the place. We had two telephones—one upstairs and one down; we would take out one of the phones. There were three light bulbs in the chandelier; two would come out. I had always put three teaspoonfuls of sugar on my oatmeal at breakfast; I would now put only one.

"These and other similar innovations in our living arrangements were discussed. She was entirely agreeable and offered full cooperation. We put the new plan into effect at once. The cook and hired man were immediately discharged; the light bulbs and one of the phones were removed. Other incidentals and rearrangements were carried out. I was not without misgivings and spent a very gloomy afternoon at home and had a rather restless night. It occurred to me (I felt possibly too late) that I had been too impulsive. It is rather sobering for a man with a wife and several children to find himself with no job and his entire income suddenly cut off.

"The next morning I came down to breakfast. My wife brought me my accustomed bowl of oatmeal. I pulled the sugar bowl over, very carefully put one teaspoonful of sugar on the cereal, and with determination pushed the bowl away. Just at that time the phone rang. I answered and found that it was Mr. Edmund F. Trabue, a distinguished Louisville lawyer and head of one of the leading law firms of the South.

"Mr. Trabue said that he had just read in the 'Courier-Journal' of my resignation from the bench and my return to private practice. He wanted to know if I was in a position to be associated with his firm in the defense of an important lawsuit that had just been filed against one of his large corporate clients. I was gratified although somewhat surprised to be offered this employment but hastily assured him that I was glad to accept.

"It was then that I received my shock. As a country lawyer in Mt. Sterling, I had known only small fees and had never had a retainer for my services. Mr. Trabue very graciously thanked me for my acceptance and said, 'Very well. I am mailing you today a check for one thousand dollars as a retainer and will discuss the amount of your fee later.'

"In something of a daze, I hung up the phone, walked

back into the dining room, pulled my chair up to the table and said, 'Pass me the sugar.'"

A fellow member of the bar and a friend of Judge O'Rear, in repeating this story many years later, added, "Yes, and they've been passing him the sugar ever since."

By way of explanation of the addendum, the Judge went on throughout his distinguished career with many affluent clients, both corporate and individual, and built an enviable and lucrative practice. It was satisfying to him and a source of gratification to his friends that he had a long life on his broad bluegrass acres in beautiful Woodford County.

* * *

Another of Judge O'Rear's stories of his life has become one of the legendary classics of the bar. The story naturally loses much of its charm when not told by the judge himself, but it is of such top quality I shall presume to record it here for fear that in the complexities of life of lawyers in future generations, it might be forever lost.

University of Camargo

The judge was engaged in the trial of a very important lawsuit in Chicago. Numerous eminent lawyers from Chicago, New York, and Detroit were representing the respective sides. The trial was prolonged and ran for several weeks. During conferences in preparation for the trial, the attorneys associated with Judge O'Rear perceived that the Kentuckian knew more about the law, the facts and method of procedure and had a greater grasp of the issues than any of his associates. He was selected to take the lead as chief counsel for his side.

By his superior knowledge, evidence of erudition and grace before the court, he soon won the respect and admiration of the judge and opposing counsel. Near the close of the trial, as a token of appreciation of his skilled advocacy, his co-counsel gave a luncheon in his honor at one of the city's exclusive clubs, to which the presiding judge and all the lawyers on both sides of the case were invited.

The convivial occasion called for renewing of friendships and acquaintances among the several attorneys present. One of these distinguished gentlemen would address another with a question such as this: "By the way, Jim, what year were you at Harvard?" To which Jim would reply, "I was Harvard '04, but I believe you were Yale '99." And another would join the conversation that he was Chicago '12 or Michigan '07, etc., etc., continuing among themselves to reminisce in a prideful if not snobbish manner by referring to the great colleges, universities, and law schools of which they were alumni.

All of this, you may be sure, was rather boring to the guest of honor who was thus entirely left out of the conversation. Finally, one of the hosts realized the situation and as there was a pause in the conversation, he turned to the Kentuckian and asked, "By the way, Judge, what is your alma mater?"

Without the slightest embarrassment or hesitation, O'Rear replied, "Camargo, gentlemen, University of Camargo."

All of those present looked at each other for a clue

and very solemnly nodded their heads, supposing it was only due to their own ignorance that none of them were familiar with, or had even heard of, the University of Camargo, the school that had as an alumnus so highly educated and eminent a scholar and lawyer. Evidently they assumed it was a great European, possibly Italian, or Spanish university. You may imagine the pleasure and amusement our friend got out of the expressions on their faces while thinking back through the years of the little, one-room, red schoolhouse, which he as a small boy had attended for about four years, back home in Kentucky near the foot of the Cumberland Mountains.

This story has become so well known that now each year at the Kentucky State Bar Association meetings there is a banquet for all alumni of symbolic Universities of Camargo who can't qualify to attend the reunions of Yale, Harvard, Kentucky or Louisville.

Importance of the law

While the law cannot be said to be an exact science, it should be acknowledged as the most important of all the sciences. This does not detract in any sense from the sciences of medicine, engineering, physics, electronics, astronomy, agriculture, pedagogy or any of the endeavors of man in his continuing effort to build a better world. All of them have contributed tremendously in our advance. It must be recognized as a fact, however, that no scientific discoveries or improvements could have been effectively brought about except in the atmosphere of an orderly society. Such a society is the business of law and lawyers.

Man can only work in any field of effort where he is protected by law and where fundamental rules of conduct are required under some form of government. We may add to this that he can achieve most in a constitutional democracy such as our own, where the protection of the dignity of the individual is the prime purpose of all law. Those who are dedicated to the law in one or more of its phases are the technicians of democracy and their obligation on the bench, before the bar, or in the classroom of a law school should be ever before them. Liberty under law must be their watchword.

When Thomas Jefferson founded the University of Virginia, he recognized the fact that the reputation of the new institution and its future success and usefulness as a seat of learning must depend on the caliber of those who composed the faculty. He wrote a letter to prospective professors and instructors in which he expressed one of his most profound thoughts.

The now famous letter contained this paragraph:

> This institution will be based on the illimitable freedom of the human mind. For here we are not afraid to follow truth wherever it may lead, nor to tolerate error so long as reason is left free to combat it.

Like Christ's parable of the merchant man, this idea is our pearl of great price. It is the one issue on which there can be no compromise. It must be accepted in its true significance or be denied. It was written by a lawyer. It is the cornerstone of all free government. It is Magna

Charta, the Declaration of Independence, Bill of Rights and Four Freedoms in one terse assertion.

Dedication of the Kentucky lawyer

Those bearing the name of lawyer are by their profession, like plumed knights, committed to its preservation and defense in the finest sense.

A small percentage of the whole membership of the bar achieves material riches, many others become financially independent; but the great majority of those who practice in Kentucky never even approach either of these categories of economic security. They are dependent upon their everyday effort, in their offices, in the courts, on the streets and highways, practicing their profession; sometimes receiving substantial fees but most of the time representing clients who have no means with which to adequately compensate them for what they accomplish. They frequently champion unpopular causes, forever taking sides in controversy; always on the firing line and in the forefront of government and community affairs. An exacting and tiring experience, but it is a rich, colorful and useful life. The true lawyer knows but one person in the world—his client and none other. To this ideal his whole being is dedicated. My contact over the years with the lawyers of Kentucky has assured me that our bar is mindful of this paramount commission.

One of the obligations of the profession arises when a lawyer is appointed by the court to defend a person charged with crime who does not have and is unable to employ counsel. At the present time there is no provision in the law of either our state or federal government to compensate these lawyers who unselfishly accept responsibility for the defendant's cause and give time and effort as conscientiously as if receiving a substantial fee.

I have never had a lawyer decline an appointment, and only in cases where an exception was justified have I had one ask to be excused. Some of these appointments have entailed heavy duties and extended time and even expenditures of money by the attorney out of his own pocket.

In many criminal cases younger members of the bar are appointed. The opportunity not only assures the defendant the enthusiastic and undivided attention of his lawyer, frequently not hampered by other business and calls on his time, but gives the new member of the bar an opportunity to gain experience and to appear before the public. It offers him a chance to show his skill and ability. If I were a young lawyer just beginning to practice, I would make myself available to the judges of the courts in my locality as much as possible for these appointments.

All the way

In some instances, however, the case suggests to the court that an attorney of greater experience should be called upon. I recall on one occasion in Bowling Green, a defendant was charged with bank robbery; he was totally without friends or funds. The nature of the case was such that I knew he would very likely receive a substantial sentence if convicted. I have always considered former Lieutenant Governor Rodes K. Myers of the Bowling Green bar one of the outstanding criminal lawyers of this state. He was generally recognized for his ability as a trial lawyer and had had wide and varied experience. There was associated with him at the time an able young lawyer, Mr. George Boston. I appointed Mr. Myers and Mr. Boston to defend the bank robber.

Two days were consumed in the trial. No accused ever received a more skillful and thorough defense, but the evidence for the government was overwhelming. The defendant was found guilty by the jury and sentenced to twenty-five years in the penitentiary. Wishing to exhaust all efforts in behalf of their client, the attorneys appealed the case, wrote briefs, appeared before the United States Court of Appeals for the Sixth Circuit at Cincinnati and argued their client's cause. Cincinnati is more than two hundred and fifty miles from Bowling Green, and the trip required an overnight stay. The attorneys paid their own expenses which, in this instance, it can be seen were quite an item.

Amicus curiae

One of the best accounts of an attorney's unselfish service to an indigent defendant comes from Honorable H. Church Ford, United States Judge for the Eastern District of Kentucky. Judge Ford was a Kentucky circuit judge before his appointment to the federal bench in 1935 by President Franklin D. Roosevelt.

While on the state bench and when holding a term of court at Frankfort, the judge had appear before him a man from the Craw section of the city of Frankfort. The

charge was wilful murder. Craw was a slum section of our
capital city where many of the families of prisoners confined in the state penitentiary had moved from other parts
of the state in order to be "near their man."

A cursory examination of the indictment and inquiry
into the surrounding facts of the homicide disclosed to
Judge Ford that the defendant was in very serious trouble.
He was not a resident of Frankfort or even of Kentucky
but was a West Virginian who had followed a family from
eastern Kentucky to Frankfort and was in town only temporarily. The altercation out of which the killing occurred
seemed to have been of his own making for the sole purpose of disposing of an adversary in a romance triangle.

The defendant, without money or friends, appeared
before the court for arraignment and entered a plea of not
guilty. He, of course, neither had a lawyer nor knew any
of the members of the Frankfort bar, so he requested that
an attorney be appointed to defend him.

Judge Ford, with some knowledge of the charges and
type of evidence that the Commonwealth would very
likely offer, was afraid the jury might give the defendant
the extreme penalty of death in the electric chair. For that
reason, he felt that he should call upon an attorney of
ability and long experience in trial work.

One of the leaders of the Kentucky bar, a man of
large practice in civil as well as criminal cases, and a very
busy lawyer, was Mr. Leslie Morris of Frankfort. Judge
Ford knew what a sacrifice it would be for Mr. Morris
to assume the defense in this criminal case—the effort
and anxiety it would place upon his shoulders and the
altogether possible disastrous outcome. He felt, however,

that the precarious position of the defendant called for
extreme measures and thereupon asked Mr. Morris if he
would accept the appointment as counsel for this friend-
less man.

The distinguished attorney arose magnificently to the
occasion and, representative of the finest traditions of our
profession, assured the judge that he would serve his client and the court to the best of his ability. The first thing
he did was to move for a continuance in order to give
himself time to make adequate preparation for the trial.
The motion was granted.

Mr. Morris postponed his other business, went into
the case carefully, took a trip to West Virginia at his own
expense, and did whatever was otherwise required, irrespec-
tive of cost to himself in money and time. He conducted
the defense at the trial as the earnest, skillful advocate that
he was.

There were numerous witnesses and the Commonwealth, represented by an able prosecutor, presented an
almost perfect case of wilful, premeditated murder. Les
Morris, an old hand in the trial of jury cases with years of
experience before the bench, fought back, yielding nothing in his zeal for his client's cause. The trial resulted in
a verdict of guilty and a penalty of life imprisonment.
Judge Ford was of the opinion that but for Mr. Morris'
fulfillment of his promise to "do his best" the verdict
would have been different. Had the defendant been less
ably represented, his life must most assuredly have been
forfeited.

* * *

Another story which I think is indicative of the caliber of lawyer Leslie Morris represents came from the late Xen Hicks, Senior Judge of the United States Court of Appeals for the Sixth Circuit at Cincinnati. Judge Hicks said that on an occasion many years ago the case of Coca Cola Company v. John Doe was on appeal from a decision against the plaintiff on an alleged trademark infringement. The case was of great significance to the plaintiff as the corporation was afraid of a precedent.

Judge Hicks said that when the court was seated he looked down at the counsel table of the plaintiff and saw distinguished lawyers from New York, Atlanta, Chicago and Detroit, a corps of at least six of the top corporation lawyers in the country. He then glanced at the defendant's table and saw sitting there all alone a "little round man." The judge said it went through his mind, "well, these giants will soon eat that little fellow up."

He said, however, as soon as "the little round man" addressed the court, he evidenced that he was well able to take care of himself with his knowledge of the law of the case and the theory on which he asked a judgment for his client. His forceful argument more than matched that of his adversaries, and the case was decided in his favor. I heard Judge Hicks tell this David and Goliath story on many occasions, always to the delight of his audience and to the everlasting credit of Mr. Morris.

Boredom

Many of the humorous stories on lawyers come from the lawyer who may himself be the butt of the joke. One of these classics is from the late United States Senator Joe C. S. Blackburn of Versailles. As the story goes, when Senator Blackburn was a very young lawyer he announced his candidacy for the office of county attorney of Woodford County. He was opposed by another ambitious young man, and Blackburn seemed to be getting the worst of it.

While the race was in progress, Joe was employed by a young defendant who had been indicted for murder. A trial was had and Joe's client was sentenced to be hanged in front of the courthouse. On the morning of the hanging it occurred to young Blackburn that since there would be a big crowd in town to witness the hanging it would be a good time for him to make a campaign speech in behalf of his candidacy.

He hurried to the jail to see his client, who, being within about an hour and a half of his demise, was in very low spirits, and the young lawyer was hesitant to broach the true purpose of his visit. He referred to and with condolences recalled the trial, how "unfair" the jury had been and how "inconsiderate" the judge had been in denying a new trial and finally lead up to the point.

"Bill," he said, "it looks like it's about all over, doesn't it?"

"Yeah, Joe," said Bill, "I reckon they ain't nothin' we kin do now."

"Well," said the young lawyer, "I just been thinking. You remember that fifty dollars you promised me to defend you, don't you?"

"Yes," answered the prisoner, "I remember it, Joe, and I'm sorry but I just ain't got no money and it looks like now I'll never have a chance to git none."

Joe extended his hand. "Well, pardner," he said, "I'm going to tell you how you can pay it and that'll be one debt you won't have to answer for on 'yon side the Jordan River."

"How's that, Joe?" the condemned man asked. "I'd sure like to clear it up with you if I could."

The young politician's enthusiasm rose and he laid out the plan. "Now, Bill, just before they put the hood over your head and the rope around your neck, the sheriff will ask if you have anything to say and you will be given time to make any statement you want to." He stopped with the query, "You don't want to say anything, do you?"

"No, Joe, I ain't got nothin' to say. I kilt the man and that's all they are to it."

"Bill," said Joe, "if you will give me that time and when they ask you just say, 'I want my attorney to say a few words,' we'll call the debt square. What do you say?"

"Agreed," said Bill. And he and his lawyer shook hands for the last time.

Some might question the good taste and propriety of trying to capitalize for votes on the occasion of a public hanging, but our novice politician thought it would be a golden opportunity. Possibly he conceived the idea that the electorate of Woodford County would be impressed with the sight of what happened to criminals when he was in the case and deduce that he would be the candidate to elect to a prosecutor's office.

Promptly on the hour the prisoner was led to the scaffold and all readings of final judgments and orders and strict observing of the proprieties of a hanging were carried out. Just before placing the hood over the prisoner's head, the sheriff asked in a loud but somewhat emotional voice, "Does the prisoner have anything he would like to say before his execution? He has the privilege of speaking at this time."

With this, Bill, who was much calmer and more self-possessed than his executioner, said, "Mr. Sheriff, I would like for my attorney, Mr. Joseph Blackburn, to say a few words at this time."

Joe stepped to the front of the platform and launched into a full-blown political harangue in the interest of his candidacy for county attorney. The crowd was somewhat taken by surprise, but as most of them had never seen a hanging before, they assumed the preliminaries to the main event could be tolerated in anticipation of the felicitous spectacle of seeing a fellow creature put to death.

In a few minutes the speaker felt a pull at his coattail; he turned his head, and Bill asked, "Joe, are you about through?"

He replied, "Not quite, Bill," and proceeded with his address.

In about ten minutes, he felt another tug at his coat. He turned his head and again Bill whispered, "Ain't you about done?"

"No, Bill, no, don't bother me like that. I'll be through in a few minutes." Blackburn again plunged into his speech, apparently oblivious to the fact that the crowd was getting bored and a little restless.

The third time a tug came on his coat. Somewhat vexed, he turned to his former client and said, "What do you want, Bill?"

And Bill, who could sense the aesthetic temper of the

crowd better than his lawyer, and, as any other star performer in a big show might feel, said, "Joe, let's let 'um go on and hang me and then you can finish your speech. You're goin' t' lose votes, and I'm gittin' tard astandin' here."

Juries usually arrive at correct decision

Many times cases take a turn that could not possibly have been anticipated by any of the participants, and yet there is very infrequently a real miscarriage of justice. Occasionally, however, there is a mistake in what issue is to be decided by the jury and for that matter by the judge. Jurors have to be informed by the attorneys and the court on what the issues to be decided are. Nothing can be taken for granted.

I have always been of the opinion that if a case was properly presented by both sides, the jury would reach a correct verdict eighty-five percent of the time, and that is about as good a percentage as a judge or group of judges makes. Too frequently poor jury lawyers condemn juries when they themselves, because of lack of ability to present their client's cause properly, are entirely at fault.

I recall a renowned railroad lawyer in one of our Kentucky cities who continually damned and condemned the jury system and juries in particular as being "stupid," prejudiced against corporations, especially railroads, and wholly incapable of reaching a fair decision on a set of facts. This attorney was a gentleman of the highest ethics and character; he was well trained in the law and prepared his cases carefully but usually had substantial verdicts in damages returned against his client in tort actions. The reason was not a lack of either intelligence or integrity of the jurors but his own fault. He tried many cases. The first thing he did by inference was to impress the jury with his deep resentment against them and his belief that so stupid and corrupt a lot of people could not be either understanding or honest. He talked down to them from first to last and reaped the consequences of his own vanity and lack of psychological know-how.

It is rare but even more reprehensible for an attorney to try to curry favor with the jurors by smirking and smiling at them and by obviously attempting in his own small mind to be just like these "plain good people" who have been put on the case to determine the rights of his client. A competent trial lawyer will treat the jury with respect but with formality as honest men and women who are trying to discharge the high duty to which their government has called them.

Many of the so-called "old time lawyers" would have made great Shakespearean actors. They could dramatize a situation in a masterful and compelling way and actually sway juries away from the case and have them trying some collateral issue which had no bearing whatsoever on the controversy.

In a western Kentucky town some years ago, a case involving a charge of slander had reached the final arguments. One of the attorneys in his closing argument asked the jury in considering the case to bear in mind the immortal words of Shakespeare: "Who steals my purse steals trash; 'tis something, nothing; 'Twas mine, 'tis his, and has been slave to thousands: But he that filches from me my good name robs me of that which not enriches him, and makes me poor indeed."

His opponent whose argument followed said that it was apparent that the gentleman who preceded him knew no more about Shakespeare than he did about the case; that it wasn't Shakespeare who had said that but Jesus Christ. He concluded his speech and the jury retired to consider the case. They remained out for an unreasonable time and finally the judge told the sheriff to bring them before him. When the jury filed in the judge inquired of the foreman what was the trouble and if there were any further instructions they might like for him to give to clarify the issue.

The foreman replied that he believed the jury was hopelessly hung; "half of them say Shakespeare and half of them say Christ."

* * *

The stubbornness of a single juror is highlighted by the following: On the occasion of a trial in a central Kentucky state court, the jury had been considering a case for several hours. Time for court to adjourn for the day had passed and the judge became restless. He said to the sheriff, "Go to the jury room and ask them if they want me to send up twelve chicken dinners." The sheriff retired but quickly returned into court. "Judge," he said, "the foreman said to thank you and have you send up eleven chicken dinners and one bale of hay."

Wrong man on trial

It is a recognized practice of skillful criminal lawyers to put the prosecuting witnesses on trial in order to get the jury's mind off the action of the defendant. These artists of rhetoric and masters of deception will cross-examine the witnesses presented by the prosecution and attempt to discredit their testimony by inference and innuendo and have the jury completely confused as to who is the offender.

It is said that Mr. W. A. Daugherty, a leading criminal lawyer in the upper Big Sandy valley for half a century, was so skillful in this respect that on one occasion he so dramatized the evil character of the chief prosecuting witness that the jury returned a verdict sending the witness to the penitentiary for fifteen years. This is only one of the many stories that have come down through the years of the prowess and exploits of the striking personalities among Kentucky lawyers. Sometimes I have felt their trenchant language and resourcefulness would not be tolerated by our modern judges.

No kiss for Uncle Harry

One of these actors of an earlier day was the Honorable Andrew Harrison Ward of the Cynthiana bar in the latter part of the nineteenth century. Uncle Harry, as he was affectionately called in Cynthiana and other central Kentucky towns where he practiced, was truly a giant of the old school in forensic debate before a jury. My father said he was the greatest natural lawyer he had ever known. He was the member of a prominent family, well educated in the profession and steeped in the classics.

He was of short, stocky stature, with massive head and shoulders. A heavy beard, a model of masculinity of that day, covered the lower part of his face and added mystery and depth to his prepossessing appearance. He carried a long cane or kind of staff which was used for emphasis in talking to people on the streets and even before juries. He had no office but used the chambers of another of Cynthiana's leading lawyers, Judge J. Quincy Ward, a distant cousin.

I was only four years old when he died so do not remember him, but from descriptions I have heard and pictures I have seen of this legendary figure, I am of the impression he gave the appearance of Socrates, the ancient Athenian sage. One of the best stories that has come down about his celebrated courthouse exploits is an account of his resourcefulness before a jury at the trial of a murder case in Paris, Kentucky.

It seems that a very outstanding young man of a prominent and wealthy Bourbon County family, in an altercation over the hand of a beautiful Kentucky belle, had shot and killed one of his contemporaries, the son of another wealthy and prominent Bourbon County family. The indictment charged him with wilful murder, and he appeared to be in such serious trouble that his conviction might result in his being hanged for the crime.

With wealth on each side, the families of both the defendant and the deceased employed the ablest counsel available. The defendant was represented by about half of the members of the Bourbon County bar and as added assurance of a complete defense the Honorable W. C. P. Breckinridge of Lexington, then a member of Congress, was employed for the defense. Mr. Breckinridge was conceded to be the most eloquent orator of his day. He had served the "Old Ashland" District in the lower house of Congress for many years. Mr. Ward, while not of such statewide prominence, was believed to be the peer of any member of the profession; so the family of the deceased, with permission of the Commonwealth, and not to be outdone, had employed him to assist the prosecution.

With two such gladiators, and the heat and excitement such a trial naturally engenders in a rural county in Kentucky, the courtroom was packed with spectators at each session of the court. After several days of trial, the case came to the closing arguments of counsel for the respective sides. Mr. Breckinridge for the defense arose to address the jury, fittingly and immaculately attired for the occasion. He was very impressive with his snow white hair and beard, ruddy complexion and erect carriage. He spoke for two hours and in his peroration said:

"Gentlemen of the jury, I have come to the close of my remarks to you; nevertheless, I am reluctant to leave you, for I realize that when I resume my seat at the counsel table, the last word in behalf of this young man will have been uttered. I feel that his innocence of this fearful crime shines like a beacon light to guide you in your deliberations. Never in my many years of experience at the bar of our state and our sister states, in the innumerable trials of cases of this character in which I have been privileged to participate have I felt so grave a responsibility as in this hour.

"I spent a sleepless night in contemplation and fear of this moment. Not in fear of the just verdict of innocence which an inner voice kept prompting me you would return into this court, but the fear of mortal man. A fear that possibly, because of some frailty of the mind on my part, some oversight for which I alone could be responsible, you had been misled or the true facts had not been made clear to you. Please, gentlemen, if such be the case, lay that sin to my charge and let it not prompt you to shed this innocent blood.

"At dawn I arose from my bed; I went to the window and looked out upon the glorious Kentucky May morning. I beheld our beloved bluegrass countryside in her party dress. Somehow the blooming flowers, the singing birds, the budding trees reassured me. I made my toilet and went down the stairs to a delicious breakfast prepared for me by my good wife, and there at the foot of the stairs I met my son, just the age of this handsome young defendant. He kissed me and said, 'Father, go there today and plead with the jurors with all the skill you possess that they send that innocent boy back to his mother, back to the loved ones who await so anxiously his return home.'

"I gave my promise. I have done my best. I leave you now. The responsibility of this boy's life is in your hands. As it seems right and good for you to do unto him, do."

Such eloquence from so impressive an orator was, as you may know, most effective. A woman in the audience sobbed; the defendant was pale and appeared on the verge of fainting. The judge on the bench and the attorneys for both sides looked very sober indeed; the jurors were entranced. Some of them had tears in their eyes. Then Uncle Harry Ward stood up and with his long hickory cane in hand, stalked to the space before the jury box. He stood very still without saying a word for a full minute, as if waiting for the entire effect of his opponent's magic to subside.

You could have heard a proverbial pin drop. The jurors and all present felt the power of his presence and knew that another great dramatist was at hand and fully in possession of the situation. He began with a loud thump of his cane on the floor. This broke the spell.

"Gentlemen," he said, "This morning I got up. I went to the window and looked out and saw the birds, the bees, the flowers and the grass." The obvious burlesque and mimicry began to take effect and get through to the jurors. Some of them smiled. A titter was heard in the back of the courtroom.

"I made my toilet by washing my face and hands and combing my beard. My wife had prepared me a good breakfast and I went downstairs to eat it. There at the foot of the stairs I met my son, just the age of that poor boy who lies buried out there in the graveyard because he was murdered by the defendant. But God bless your souls, gentlemen, if he'd kissed me, I'd have knocked hell out of him."

For the next few minutes it was almost impossible to restore order in to courtroom. The partisans of the prosecution laughed out loud and even the judge, rapping with his gavel for order, could hardly suppress a smile. I can only conclude this story by confessing that I have never heard how the jury decided. It does, however, illustrate how a clever and bold trial lawyer can bring a sudden and sometimes effective change in the fortunes of his client when the tide appears to be going steadily against him.

The case of the diamond ring

A striking incident of this was demonstrated in the federal court at Pikeville on one occasion. Without reciting all the details of the case, the trial had reached a place where the former wife of the defendant in a civil action was testifying. The action was in the nature of discovery to establish title to property which the defendant was supposed to have owned and which he was alleged to have transferred to his present wife in order to avoid paying a substantial judgment.

The defendant was sitting at the counsel table with his attorney, Mr. Ervin Sanders, of the Pikeville bar. His wife, a very comely young blonde, was seated beside him. She was wearing a large diamond ring which had attracted some attention from the court attaches and spectators for the two days of the trial. The witness, who I have said was the former wife of the defendant and was, of course, hostile to the defendant, had been subpoenaed to testify about the disposition of the property. Among other things she said that her former husband had bought and given to her a twelve thousand dollar diamond ring which he had required her to return to him when they separated. She gave a very minute description of the ring and its setting. She related very convincingly the reason she knew its value and the fact that she herself had seen it paid for with thousand dollar bills taken from a safety vault tin box. She then said, "That's the ring right there on his wife's hand now."

This remark seemed to take by surprise the attorney who had called her as a witness. It was indeed a valuable bit of evidence. The attorney enlarged upon it and had her reiterate the details of the acquisition of the ring and its positive value. Finally, he concluded his examination and sat back to enjoy the discomfort and vexation of opposing counsel.

Mr. Sanders cross-examined the witness on many other matters, unrelated to the incident of the ring. It appeared as if he were going to ignore it as the best way out of a bad situation. The wearer of the ring made no effort to conceal it but left it in plain view for everyone to admire. At last, Mr. Sanders asked the witness to again recount the reasons, background and steps by which and for which the ring had been acquired and paid for by the defendant.

This she gladly did, seeming to get unusual pleasure out of publicly ridiculing her successor in their husband's affection as the belated possessor of her own cast off, second-hand jewelry. I don't know just how far a twelve thousand dollar jewel can become a thing to be disdained by a second wife. Finally, after repeated positive identification, Mr. Sanders took the ring from the wearer and walked to the witness chair and handed it to the witness.

"Now," he said, "are you positive that is the ring?"

"Yes," was the prompt reply.

"It is the same stone and the same setting?"

"Exactly," came from the witness.

He then took the ring and turned his back on the witness as if to return to his counsel table. After a few steps he turned again and went back to her.

"I do not want to be persistent, but I want you to again carefully examine this ring which you say you once wore for several months and tell this court whether you have the slightest doubt of its being your ring, or rather, the one which your husband paid twelve thousand dollars for."

She again took the ring in her hand and more positively than ever reaffirmed her identification.

The lawyer then took it from her, walked to opposing counsel's table and laid it down in front of him with the remark, "You can have it; it cost two dollars and twenty-five cents."

Everyone was stunned. All of us had been completely taken in. I have never learned the true state of facts about this ring. I believed the witness was telling the truth. I could not make inquiry of Mr. Sanders as I was trying the case. If some day the mystery of the twelve thousand dollar ring is revealed, I may yet learn what happened.

The opposing attorney was, of course, disappointed because he did not get an opportunity to subject this valuable asset as a credit on his judgment.

Battle of San Juan Hill

The following story, while not exactly identified with the profession, is about one of the most important functionaries and office holders in the legal system, the county jailer. These men of each community are almost in a class by themselves. As a rule they are rather vivid personalities whose chief claim to qualification for office is their wide acquaintanceship and friendly nature. Formerly it was not a bad office to hold. The emoluments included a house to live in, a steady income from the county for the care and maintenance of the courthouse and a per diem for all prisoners. I can recall several years ago at election time in my county, there were always as many as five and sometimes eight and ten candidates for the office.

The subject of our story is the late Fes Whitaker of Whitesburg, Letcher County, Kentucky. Fes was well known and well liked throughout that eastern Kentucky county. He had served as jailer of his county for four years and was running for re-election. He had stiff opposition and his resourcefulness was being put to a severe test. He, however, appeared equal to it. The mountain section of Kentucky in those days was overwhelmingly Republican in political complexion, and Fes, as a staunch partisan of the Republican faith, identified himself with the late, colorful and popular Theodore Roosevelt. According to Whitaker, he and Teddy had been bosom friends in the United States Army during the Spanish-American War. They had bunked together in Cuba and were inseparable. Then, as now, and I suppose as ever, military service enhanced a candidate's chances of being elected and emphasis was placed upon the slightest evidence of heroic sacrifice and service under the flag.

Fes exploited his career as a soldier and closeness to the former Republican president to the fullest. He gathered crowds around him and told of their hardships together. Then he would come to the climax of his story. "I shall never forget," he would say, "the day of the Battle of San Juan Hill. Teddy and I in our pup tent had spent a sleepless night. We knew that our country's honor was at stake and would likely be determined on the following day. On the morning of the battle the lines were quickly drawn, supporting cannon was heard from our Navy in the bay. The enemy advanced, but our lines held and then came the bayonet charge of our soldiers and the break in the ranks of the Spaniards. The retreat became a run and finally a disorganized rout. Teddy and I, side by side, our horses neck and neck, galloped up San Juan Hill. When we reached the top we could see the enemy fleeing toward the sea with our men in hot pursuit and we knew that the day was won and victory was ours. Suddenly I saw Teddy jump from his horse. I followed suit. There lying on the ground before us was the flag, our American flag that had been trampled under the feet of the disposed enemy. Teddy picked it up and secured it to the flag pole and together we raised it high in the air. It was a wonderful sight, my fellow citizens, to see Old Glory floating and lashing in the breeze. We stood silently and drank in the beauty of this scene for fully ten minutes. Then Teddy walked over to me, put his arm around my shoulder and said, 'Fes, this is going to make one of us President of the United States,' and I said to him, 'Yes, Teddy, I know, but you be President. All I want to be is jailer of Letcher County, Kentucky.'"

You may well guess the outcome of the jailer's race and cannot be greatly surprised that the victor was the Honorable Festus Whitaker, soldier and statesman.

The League of Nations

The jailer is many times the party wheelhorse and is powerful and useful in a very practical way in the interest of his party at election time when he is not a candidate. The late A. B. Rouse, former Congressman from the Fifth District, and who served with credit as Clerk of the United States District Court for Eastern Kentucky for many years, told this story. It was during the presidential election of 1920 when Warren G. Harding, Republican, was running against James M. Cox, Democrat. The big issue in the campaign was the League of Nations which Woodrow Wilson's administration had espoused. The Democrats had adopted a League plank in their platform and were forced to protect it against a very effective assault by isolationists concentrated behind the Republican nominee. The Kenton County Democratic Committee was winding up its campaign with a big picnic and rally at Independence. The main speaker was Circuit Judge Harbison of Covington who spoke for two hours, principally extolling the virtues of the League of Nations and the obligation of Americans to support it by electing a Democratic president. Mr. Rouse was the local party treasurer. He said immediately after the speaking he called the jailer behind the courthouse and said, "Now, Jim, we're going to win, but all of us must bend every effort to get the vote to the polls. We *must* get the vote out." While so speaking he slipped seventy-five one dollar bills into the jailer's hand. Jim looked at the roll of greenbacks. "Mr. Rouse," he said, "you have thrown more light on the League of Nations in the last two minutes than Matt Harbison has in the past two hours."

The prohibition era

In the days of national prohibition, in what is now referred to as the roaring twenties, the federal courts were crowded with cases growing out of violations of the generally unpopular law. Racketeers and gangsters, with money derived from the illicit liquor traffic, conducted an invisible government. Law enforcement was confronted with the most difficult, if not impossible, task of any time in the history of our land, either before or since.

The most celebrated hoodlum was "Scar Face" Al Capone, a thug whose headquarters were in Chicago. This king of vice and crime, it was said, had his henchmen, bootleggers, rum runners and killers throughout the whole United States and some of our island possessions. I give this background for the benefit of those who are not old enough to remember the famous era of American prohibition.

Mr. Cleon Calvert was a distinguished lawyer of Pineville. He was recognized as a capable land lawyer and had for many years been retained by Henry Ford as his attorney in eastern Kentucky to look after the Ford interests in minerals and timber located in that area. Mr. Calvert did not practice criminal law but was a regular attendant on the first day of the term of the London federal court to hear the civil docket called and the assignment for trial of civil cases in which he was interested.

He said that on one occasion after the call of the civil docket he sat in the courtroom waiting on a fellow Pineville attorney to return home and while so occupied became interested as an observer in the disposition of the criminal docket. One case in particular attracted his attention. Two very fine looking young men were on trial for stealing from an interstate shipment of freight. The cargo was a truck load of legal whiskey being transferred from one warehouse to another. The youths protested their innocence but had no counsel except a very young and inexperienced lawyer whom the court had appointed for them.

The issue was one of identity. The government rested its whole case upon the testimony of the Negro driver of the truck who stated that, although the holdup was at night, he positively recognized the defendants by the light of a flashlight and when they walked within the glare of the headlights of the truck. The jury accepted the witness' story and found the boys guilty. Judge Cochran sentenced them to five years in the penitentiary.

Mr. Calvert said when he went home that night, he couldn't get the two young defendants off of his mind. He was positive the jury had made a mistake. The boys were so young and clean-cut looking and had protested their innocence so vigorously. On the other hand, he knew that the driver, under all the circumstances of the holdup, would have been too frightened to have been able in so short a time to positively record in his mind the identity of those making the holdup. He was so concerned that he drove the fifty miles back to London the next morning and interviewed the judge. He told Judge Cochran that he had not practiced a criminal case for many years but he felt he owed it to the court and to his profession to try to right a miscarriage of justice. He offered his services to assist the inexperienced young lawyer or to take full responsibility for the case if the judge would give those two young boys another trial.

The judge was not too impressed with Mr. Calvert's conviction of the innocence of the prisoners but he could not decline such insistence and granted a new trial. A vigorous defense resulted in an acquittal on the second trial and the boys were released. Calvert felt very grateful. His clients were overjoyed. They wanted his address and told him they hoped later to be able to pay him a substantial fee. He very graciously declined and said that he was so convinced of their innocence that he was fully compensated by the feeling that he had prevented a gross miscarriage of justice. They insisted, however, that he give them his card and thanking him profusely for his friendship they left the court.

In about thirty days Mr. Calvert said he went to the postoffice and found in his box a very long and interesting looking envelope. He opened it to find it contained a check for twenty-five hundred dollars signed "Al Capone."

The Purchase

One of the most delightful and interesting parts of the state of Kentucky is the far western portion known as the Jackson Purchase. The Purchase needs no word from me to recall its charm and rich historical background and the tremendous contribution its native sons have made to the dignity and glory of our state in all fields. Such names as Irvin S. Cobb and Alben W. Barkley would lead a list of numerous distinguished men and women whose names readily come to mind.

Since I have referred to the two prize storytellers and platform or literary entertainers, it may appear that I have covered the field. That is not so. All great people are not discovered by historians and all vivid personalities do not reach the general public attention. I am reminded of what Bob Zuppke, famous Illinois coach, said about all-American football players and what it took to make them stand out above many others of equal if not superior ability, "weak opposition and a poet in the press box." I firmly believe that most men and women of great historical notoriety have had a "poet in the press box," while many who made equal or greater contributions to their times were less fortunate in this respect and have gone comparatively unnoticed.

In the many weeks of holding court at Paducah, especially from 1938 to 1940, I had the most pleasant contact with members of the bar, their families and friends. I shall never forget the courtesies shown me and the efforts made to make my stay enjoyable. The Honorable Bunk Gardner, Sr. from Mayfield was United States Attorney. He was a past master as a storyteller and entertainer. Full of wit and rich experiences, Judge Gardner was delightful company. He had had a very full career. He was born and reared in Graves County; practiced law in Mayfield for several years; filled various county and judicial district offices, including that of circuit judge; and was finally appointed attorney for the Reconstruction Finance Corporation at Washington, D.C. Later he became United States Attorney for the Western District of Kentucky from which office he resigned to accept appointment as United States Judge for the Canal Zone.

Cost of love

Judge Gardner told me of his first trial as a state circuit judge. The first term of court he held after taking office was at Bardwell in Carlisle County and the first civil case on the docket was an action to recover damages for breach of promise. The plaintiff was represented by two of Kentucky's more respected and revered attorneys, Judge J. E. Robbins and Judge Gus Thomas of Mayfield. The defendant was represented by Mr. John Shelbourne, a prominent lawyer of western Kentucky and father of U.S. District Judge Roy M. Shelbourne of Louisville. The plaintiff, a local schoolteacher, had made the fatal mistake of falling in love with one of her pupils of the high school senior class. Fortunately, or possibly unfortunately, her love was reciprocated and a clandestine romance grew and flourished for the last half of the school year. She was of some attraction but about nine years older than her pupil and lover.

After graduation, the pent-up feelings of this twenty-eight-year-old teacher and her nineteen-year-old beau came out in the open and an active and aggressive courtship took place, somewhat to the disgust of the populace of the small community. When the next school year rolled around the young man went to Louisville Medical School and his sweetheart continued with her teaching. Throughout his college career their affection quickened and, with the summers for courtship and correspondence while the young man was at college, grew into an engagement of marriage to be consummated at some distant date after the embryo doctor had established himself in his profession.

When his medical college course was completed, he was licensed to practice and opened an office in his home town. Needless to say his maturity had developed him into a very attractive and good-looking young professional man. The years had not been so kind to his fiancee. She had passed the bloom of girlhood and now in her middle thirties was bordering on what was called in those days an old maid, a phrase which I hasten to renounce as unjust and unkind and one that should be stricken from our lexicon. The courtship, however, continued throughout another year.

The young doctor had acquired patients on whom to practice and was well on his way to success. The wedding bells were not far distant and the nuptials were about to take place when suddenly the whole plan, arrangement and dream was upset by the appearance on the scene of a rival for the old maid schoolteacher. One of the local girls had been away to college and had brought home for a visit her roommate, a very pretty girl of about twenty years of age. The young doctor had met her at a social function and apparently it was one of those love-at-first-sight affairs. Without delay the young couple was married.

The old maid sweetheart promptly filed suit against her former pupil and erstwhile future husband for breach of promise, claiming ten thousand dollars for a broken heart, wounded pride and irreconcilable grief.

Jury lawyers are born, not made. Gus Thomas and Judge Robbins were born jury lawyers. Without breach of ethics or being subject to criticism, they knew how to dramatize their case and how to win. The setting was perfect for their combined talents. At the beginning of the case and at each recess they practiced the art of perfect timing. When the jury was seated in the jury box the handsome young defendant, well groomed and successful looking, with his beautiful young wife, dressed in the fashion of the day, with shapely legs covered by silk stockings and a stylish slinging dress, came in and were seated at the counsel table. When everything was in readiness, there appeared from the farthest entrance to the courtroom the plaintiff's attorneys with their client, properly dressed for full effect. She was very tall, very thin, and very pale. She had undoubtedly been coached to wear a long, black dress which reached almost to her ankles, black shoes, and to carry a very white, small handkerchief. This severe attire had the effect of accentuating the plaintiff's height, slimness and pallor. Frequently she would touch her eyes with the white handkerchief.

Her lawyers had lying on the counsel table several bundles of letters, tied with pink and blue ribbon, from which they read to the jury ardent love passages in which the homesick young college boy had poured out his soul to his betrothed back home. Finally the case was concluded and submitted to the jury. In less than thirty minutes the jury returned a verdict for the plaintiff for three thousand dollars, a substantial sum in those days in that locality.

The court was adjourned for the day and Judge Gardner left the courtroom, walking a few feet behind Mr. Shelbourne. When they reached the street it was noticed that one of the jurors was walking in the direction of his saddle mule which was tied to the courthouse hitching rack. Judge Gardner said Mr. Shelbourne appeared very much vexed at the loss of his case. He caught up with the juror and the judge heard him say, "Jim, what in the world could you jurors have been thinking of to give such a large verdict?" The juror, who with his fellow jurors had been observing and comparing the young wife of the doctor and the old maid plaintiff for two and a half days, answered promptly and with some feeling, "Now, Mr. Shelbourne, you know damn well there's more than three thousand dollars difference between them two women."

A plea for mercy

Judge Gardner said he had had the honor of holding many political offices, among them county attorney, circuit judge, attorney for the R. F. C. and United States Attorney, but he believed the most interesting of all and the one he enjoyed most was the office of Police Judge of Mayfield. He pointed out that in that capacity he saw a full cross-section of crime in rural America and had more opportunity to study psychology firsthand than at any time in his life. He said as an example, there was a well-known local police court character by the name of George Bray, with whom he had grown up on the streets of Mayfield. George was one of those rare individuals who was born to greatness but who, because of a complete lack of application and effort, and indulgence in alcoholic beverages, let his talents atrophy and became in his early adult life a bum.

When he was growing up George had been the town and school hero in athletics. He was a natural in anything of a physical nature he undertook. He could run faster, pitch and hit better, jump higher and broader, and excelled all others in any kind of a contest. Because of his former supremacy he was tolerated far beyond his deserts in his lawless escapades. He would get drunk regularly on alternate Saturday nights, beat up his wife, run his children out of the house and break up the furniture. His wife would swear out a warrant for him, but as soon as George sobered up and had an opportunity to talk to her, she would come to the officials and beg them to drop the charges. George was always remorseful and never tried to defend his conduct. And as a result of his former popularity and deep remorse, and the further fact that any costs or fines assessed would have to be paid by his wife out of meager earnings from a poorly paying job in a local dry goods store, the charges would be dropped.

Judge Gardner said one Monday morning at the regular police court call of the docket, he noticed George at the foot of the line, standing with his great athletic shoulders slumping and head bowed in a remorseful and self-pitying way. He noticed the police report and saw that on the Saturday night before George had gotten on one of his accustomed bi-monthly drunks and had beaten his wife, run his children out of the house and broken the few remaining pieces of furniture which the house contained.

The judge said he thought if he would change the charge from the customary accusation of drunkenness and disorderly conduct to something with a higher and more important sound, there was hope that it might have a deterrent effect upon his wayward boyhood chum, so summoning all the vitriol which only a police judge possesses and the skill of a trained prosecutor, using all legal verbiage at his command, he read the charge which concluded with the words, "I charge you with a *breach of the peace* and fine you one hundred dollars." These words "breach of the peace" were uttered with a snarl and emphasis far beyond their true significance. Nevertheless, it seemed to work. George had never heard the term before notwithstanding his frequent appearances in court. Judge Gardner said he eyed George with all of the coldness and contempt he could muster. The culprit slowly raised his head and looked at him through blood-shot eyes and said in a thick voice, "Judge, would you mind commutin' that to life sentence?"

Trial of prohibition violators

Prohibition had its staunch adherents and its open violators. It was a failure but not because of the attitudes of either of these extremes. The weakness of the law was inherent. Whatever popularity it enjoyed at the height of the experiment was short lived. The people generally of all sections of our country finally lost respect for it and it became almost impossible to get a conviction of violators either in the state or federal courts.

I was United States Attorney for the last year of its existence and tried conscientiously to enforce the law. We had a great many cases in the Eastern District of Kentucky. This district was in fact second only to the Southern District of New York in the number of criminal cases. Most of those charged with violation in the federal court plead guilty. Some, however, entered pleas of not guilty and demanded a jury trial. If the case was a clear one, the jury would usually convict, but if there was any doubt, reasonable or imaginary, there was invariably a "hung jury." There was rarely ever an acquittal. The reason for so many hung juries is left to your imagination or wisdom. I will not hazard an explanation. Some observers were so bold as to suggest that although the violations were flagrant and universal, juries would not convict because some of the jurors very probably had "bootleg booze" at home or "home brew" in the cellar.

Each community had its particular way of breaking the prohibition law. In some places the imported whiskey was delivered to the home of the customer. In other places deliveries were made at his place of business. Still other consumers sought out their retailers at some rendezvous in the woods or down some country lane.

Santa Claus

I heard the late Judge Dick Thomas of Bowling Green tell this story of a famous lawyer of Brownsville, Edmonson County, of a generation ago. His name was Milton Wright and he was one of those delightful small town lawyers, scholars and seers, who, I must regretfully say, are rapidly passing from our scene, but who, we hope, legend will preserve for us in memory a few more years. Brownsville and its citizens of overwhelming Baptist and Methodist persuasion still jealously held on to the moral side of the law on the question of prohibition. Do not misunderstand me. This did not include all of the citizenry of that delightful little city, but the so-called "good people" so outnumbered the others that it was necessary for those who were publicly "dry" but privately "wet" to have some secret method of getting their liquor. Consequently they generally practiced the third of the above enumerated ways or what has been called the rendezvous plan.

It was Christmas Eve and the sheriff sitting watchfully in his car near the courthouse saw one of the local hypocrites leave town and drive toward a backwoods section of the county some few miles away. The sheriff was well acquainted with the section where exchanges of money for moonshine whiskey was a somewhat thriving business. Taking a short cut, he left his car and worked his way through the woods to a place near a large oak tree beside which was a small black gum stump. From a hiding place he waited for several minutes until he was rewarded by seeing the town man come down the path, look furtively about him and place three one dollar bills on the stump, then turn and walk back up the path a few paces. Almost immediately a hand and arm appeared from behind the oak, grasped the money and disappeared only to again instantly reappear and place a quart Mason jar of moonshine on the stump. The sheriff waited. The purchaser came back down the path, picked up the jar and put it under his coat just as the sheriff rushed from his hiding place.

He arrested the purchaser but was not quick enough to catch the seller. Charges were made against the embarrassed and unfortunate man accusing him of purchasing alcoholic beverages in violation of the law. Being a respected citizen and churchman he could not afford to admit his guilt by pleading guilty, though you may wonder what defense he could possibly have had. He employed Mr. Wright and in due season the case was brought to trial in the Quarterly Court at Brownsville.

The sheriff testified and gave the eyewitness account I have just stated. The Commonwealth closed its case and counsel for the defendant stated that he offered no proof and the evidence was closed. The judge gave the stereotyped written instructions proper in such cases and called for the arguments. Mr. Wright, with his thick gray hair, rosy cheeks and quaint old-fashioned dress, stood up before the jury, a picture of the natural elegance of the old school lawyer. He made a few complimentary remarks about the judge and the jury, reminding them of the grave duty which this attack upon his client's honor placed upon them, then came to the point of his speech.

"Now, gentlemen," he said to the six men occupying the chairs before him, "when you went into the jury box you didn't leave your common sense back there in the courtroom. You took it with you and when you go to your jury room to determine the fate of my client, I'm asking each one of you to use that common sense which is the basis of all law and justice. You heard the judge instruct you that before you could find the defendant guilty you must believe beyond a reasonable doubt that he *bought* that jar of whiskey. Gentlemen, remember what time of year this was and what day it was. It was the Yuletide season, Christmas Eve. That night was a time for the good saint to visit his friends over all the world. Across the sea in the great country of Germany, Kris Kringle was bringing to the little golden haired Gretchen a talking doll. In Holland, St. Nicholas was delivering in the stocking of Hans Brinker a pair of silver skates, and here in our own broad land he was likewise calling on his friends.

"Gentlemen," he said, "Gentlemen, that wasn't the hand of a bootlegger that put that whiskey on that stump . . ." Here this superb actor drew closer to the jurors and bent toward them with his hands on his knees. The jurors were fascinated and automatically leaned forward in their seats. The orator then glanced slyly over each shoulder and placing his hands cupshaped about his mouth said in a stage whisper, "it was the hand of Santa Claus." He turned and sat down.

The suppressed laughter in the court was lost on the matter of fact and entirely unimaginative young county attorney. In his speech he argued strenuously for a conviction and concluded with, "Now, gentlemen, you know that wasn't nobody but a bootlegger because there ain't no Santa Claus."

The jury took the written instructions and filed out of the court to their jury room to consider the case. In twenty minutes they returned and the foreman read the verdict: "We, the jury, find the defendant not guilty. There is a Santa Claus."

Some confusion

One of Kentucky's most illustrious sons was the Honorable John G. Carlisle of Covington. Mr. Carlisle had a distinguished career at the bar and in the public service. He practiced extensively throughout northern and central Kentucky for several years and was a friend and associate in various cases of my father who admired him so much he named his first born son for him. Mr. Carlisle served in various governmental capacities and was a member of the Cabinet as Secretary of the Treasury under President Grover Cleveland.

Notwithstanding his eminence, he had a failing which was not uncommon to the prominent and successful lawyer of that day, and, for that matter, holds over to a degree to our generation. He would on occasions imbibe too freely and was known at times to become intoxicated.

It is said that he was one of the most convincing and eloquent speakers of his day. During the heated presidential campaign of 1896, in which the free silver issue was uppermost, Mr. Carlisle was first against free silver and later for it. He is said to have made the greatest gold standard speech of the campaign when he was on that side of the debate, and, after changing, made the most effective speech in favor of free silver that was delivered during the campaign.

He was a friend of another colorful Covington lawyer, Theodore Hallam, who had some of the same convivial habits. On an evening in Covington, Mr. Carlisle, Mr. Hallam and three or four more of their lawyer friends were having a few drinks at a popular tavern. About one o'clock in the morning the bartender suggested that it was closing time and the gentlemen would have to leave. This they did without incident. Arm in arm they wended (with emphasis on the word "wended") their way homeward. They came first to Mr. Carlisle's dwelling and without thought rang the bell. Mrs. Carlisle raised an upstairs window and inquired of the group what they wanted. One of the gentlemen stated that they had brought Mr. Carlisle home. The lady said, "Very well, just open the door and put him in the hall." The quick-witted Hallam immediately responded, "Madam, I'm afraid you will have to come down and pick him out."

Lawyers and politics

Most lawyers because of their training are interested in politics. The very fact that their minds turn toward government and law as a chosen profession indicates that there is a bent to hold office or at least to participate actively in political battles for their friends or for leaders whom they admire. They are as a class militantly partisan and adhere to their own political party with dogged loyalty even when issues may turn away those of less steadfast faith. Formerly, probably to a greater extent than at present, it was looked upon as the unpardonable sin for a Democrat or Republican to desert or "bolt" his party's nominee. By such act he stigmatized himself and seriously jeopardized any future political ambitions he might have or might later acquire.

I suppose it was because of the Civil War that this feeling was at times not only deep but aroused anger and emotions that engendered a hatred that lasted for a lifetime. Kentucky, because of its geographic location, probably had this feeling among her citizens to a greater extent than any other state. The population, divided in its loyalties during the war, could hardly be expected to become otherwise in the immediate post-war period.

The governor's race of 1899 was bitterly fought and had the most tragic results of any of Kentucky's many colorful political battles. The most controversial personality that Kentucky had ever known up until that time or, for that matter, since, was the Honorable William Goebel, state senator from Kenton County. This man was the idol of a large segment but by no means a majority of the Democrats of the state. He was intelligent, forceful and loyal to his allies but above all he was possessed of a political ambition that knew no bounds. He was chosen as the Democratic nominee for governor at what is known as the famous Music Hall Convention in Louisville in the summer of 1899. The methods used to secure the nomination angered and alienated all of those who opposed him and the intense feeling of some of the delegates resulted in bringing out another Democrat to run as an independent for the office. W. S. Taylor was the Republican nominee. Since the story does not involve the many other interesting features of this never to be forgotten race, I will not go into them. If anyone who reads this is looking for Kentucky political history, I recommend *Famous Kentucky Tragedies and Trials,* by L. F. Johnson.

"Yellow dog Democrat?"

One of the chief leaders of the revolt against the nominee and therefore a "bolter" of the Democratic party was Theodore Hallam, referred to above. Mr. Hallam took the stump and campaigned vigorously against Goebel, whom he heartily disliked and distrusted. While speaking in western Kentucky he was asked by the "loyal" Democrats to divide time or share his platform with Judge John Rhea of Russellville. This was a method of debate which was for a time popular in Kentucky politics. Hallam accepted and before a large audience these two skillful political artisans eloquently extolled the virtues of their respective candidates. It was known to the crowd that Mr. Hallam had been theretofore a devout partisan and had avowed that he was so attached to his party and its principles that he would vote for a "yellow dog" on the Democratic ticket before he would vote for a Republican. This gave rise to the expression "a yellow dog Democrat" which, in a small measure, is used today.

During the progress of Hallam's speech, a heckler in the audience shouted, "I thought you said you were a yellow dog Democrat, so why are you out here leading a party bolt in favor of Republicans?" Hallam promptly replied, "You're right, I did say that I was and I am a yellow dog Democrat and will vote for a yellow dog before I will vote for a Republican, but I won't go one bit lower than a yellow dog, and that's what they are asking when they offer William Goebel as the Democratic nominee."

Two of a kind

My father was actively interested in politics throughout his long life. I have heard him say that Judge John Rhea of Russellville was the greatest political orator he had ever heard. At the time of the incident just related, he was in his prime. At the conclusion of Hallam's speech, Judge Rhea arose and addressed the crowd of wildly cheering Democrats.

"Ladies and gentlemen," he said, "you have just heard an address by one of Kentucky's most eloquent and illustrious sons. A man favored by nature to fill positions of leadership both in his profession as a lawyer and his avocation as a statesman. He is my fellow Kentuckian, my fellow Southerner, my fellow Democrat. From early youth I have known and admired this talented man. In the courtroom, on the forum, in legislative halls, I have heard him sound forth as a prophet of old, pointing the way to some proper conclusion of a legal or public question. I have gladly followed, almost blindly, his inspired and lofty leadership."

With this, John Rhea's attitude and posture changed. Gifted actor that he was he evidenced overwhelming disappointment. His shoulders sagged and his head bent slightly forward. He continued, "But, now, now my fellow Democrats, I am bowed down with a deep sorrow. A sorrow which comes in a way no other such emotion can come. It is the disappointment of one man in another for whom he has held a deep and abiding affection. A loss of faith in an ideal. My idol has been found to have feet of clay."

The speaker's demeanor changed again. He became stern and severe. His eyes flashed a fire of righteous wrath. "This man," he said, "who so boldly struts before you, parading his infidelity, shouting and breathing out threats of destruction against the great party of Jefferson and Jackson, the one best hope of the state all of us love so much, would lead you into paths of hopelessness and gloom. This man has been honored time and again by the Democratic party. Now, almost on bended knee, he begs and implores you to desert his benefactor. To defeat and ridicule your party and mine." With this conclusion the speaker's voice again changed. With perfect pitch, a shade of pathos came into it. His hearers were entranced and stood spellbound.

"Somewhere, my friends," he said, "in some unknown and distant spot—maybe on a bald mountain top, maybe in some hidden valley—but somewhere on this earth is the grave of Judas Iscariot. Immediately after this election is over, the Democratic party should appoint a committee to locate that grave and when our speaker of the afternoon comes to his final demise, the Democratic party should send his remains to that spot and bury him beside the malefactor of our Saviour and erect a joint headstone with the inscription: 'Here lies Judas: Here lies Hallam.'"

A Kentucky ghost story

No accumulation of the legends and actions of Kentuckians would be complete without a ghost story. This romantic land, with its rivers, hills, valleys and wooded bluegrass pastures, lends itself to mystery. The following story illustrates a gross miscarriage of justice and its consequences.

In the hills of eastern Harrison County in a country churchyard stands a small monument of native limestone. It is covered with moss, and the stone itself seems to have aged far more than the near century and a quarter it has marked the final resting place of a lovely young Kentucky woman. Blackened by time, its inscription is still legible:

In Memory of Nancy Ann
Daughter of J. and Nancy Maynor
Born Jan. 1, 1819
Murdered June 6, 1847

The story behind this lonely grave is tragic and yet thrilling.

David Sheely was a young farmer, and he and his wife, Nancy, lived in a two-room log cabin on Crooked Creek near where the stream flows into the Licking River. In the late afternoon of June 5, 1847, David and a group of his friends went to Beaver Creek, some distance from his home, on a fishing party. The fish were "biting," and by midnight the men had made a great catch. Unfortunately, their fishing was interspersed with frequent drams of whiskey. At about midnight the whiskey gave out and the fish quit biting. In a drunken boast, David invited the fishermen to go home with him where he said he would have his good wife, Nancy, draw and clean the fish and cook for them a fine breakfast of fish and cornbread. All of the men in a drunken condition arrived at the Sheely cabin at about two in the morning. Nancy was awakened and ordered to get dressed and to clean and cook the fish. This she positively declined to do, and an argument ensued between her and her husband. David was subjected to the ridicule of his drunken friends because he could not control his wife who persistently refused to obey him. Finally the laws of nature prevailed and the intoxicated men were overcome by sleepiness. David lay down in the bed beside his wife. The others sprawled on the floor of the cabin or on the grass in the yard outside the door.

When Sheely awoke the following morning all of the men were gone. His wife, Nancy, lay dead beside him, apparently strangled to death. A neighbor went to the house during the day and found the body of the dead woman on the bed. Her husband was nowhere to be found, and the small cabin was deserted. An alarm was given and there was great excitement which soon spread throughout the county. The sheriff formed a posse to track down the missing husband. He was discovered hiding in the chimney of the old stone fireplace in his home.

On September 14, 1847, the Harrison County grand jury returned an indictment charging David Sheely with the wilful murder of his wife, Nancy. From the dusty archives of the Harrison County Circuit Clerk's office the following entitled record is brought to light. First, tied with a neat black tape is this paper:

Commonwealth ⎱
    vs.   ⎰ Transcript of Record
David Sheely

Next:

Commonwealth ⎱
    vs.   ⎰ Murder
David Sheely
A true bill.

J. D. Thomas, Foreman
Filed 14th Sept., 1847.

The case was tried at this same September term of court before Circuit Judge Richard A. Buckner, Jr. Upon arraignment, the prisoner entered a plea of not guilty.

While the defendant had a few sympathizers, the people of the county were generally incensed over the death of an innocent young housewife as the direct result of drunken rowdyism by a bunch of ruffians brought to her home by the accused. Nancy's murder was the chief subject of discussion throughout Harrison and the adjoining counties. Public sentiment was definitely against the accused. Eliza Johnson, a twelve-year-old girl, testified that she had lived at the Sheely home for two or three weeks just before the murder. She stated that on one occasion she saw Sheely seize his wife by the throat and choke her to the floor and tell her he would see her heart's blood before morning. He had also made such threats against the little witness to the effect that he would kill her if she stayed, that she left the house and was afraid to return.

William Williams swore that he was at the Sheely home on a Saturday night shortly before the killing; that David was drinking heavily on that occasion; and that he "thought" he had heard him threaten to kill Nancy, but was not positive. A third witness, Dr. W. H. A. Worthum, testified to marks indicative of violence about the victim's neck and arms and a bruise on the elbow and hip. These wounds, the physician said, were not of themselves sufficient to produce death, "but the indentations on the left side of the throat gave evidence of violence from the right hand of the murderer by his grasping the trachea or windpipe between the thumb and finger, which was sufficient of itself to produce death of the individual by stopping respiration."

Two other witnesses, William Smith and Zedekiah Miller, testified that they were at the Sheely house after the murder was committed and that they saw the body and were of the opinion the woman had been choked to death.

The only witness who testified for the defense was the accused man. He was very reticent and in answer to all questions, both of his own counsel and on cross examination by the attorney for the Commonwealth, would make but one statement. "If I killed Nancy Sheely, I don't know it. I never had nothin' agin her."

The case was submitted to the jury for its determination and in a short while it returned into court the following verdict: "We, the jury, find the prisoner at the bar to be guilty of wilful murder as charged in the written indictment. Signed, Silas H. Sparks, foreman."

On September 30, 1847, the prisoner was brought before Judge Buckner for sentence under the verdict of the jury. The judge asked him if he had anything to say before sentence was pronounced. The condemned man, with a dull stare of hopelessness, looked at the sheriff who stood beside him, then at his attorney and finally turned his frightened gaze to the judge. He shook his tousled head and repeated the only defense he had ever claimed. "If I killed Nancy Sheely, I don't know it. I never had nothin' agin her."

He was then sentenced to be hanged on October 30. Governor William Owsley, through the importunity of some unidentified persons, granted a stay of execution until November 19. David was again placed in the county jail in the death cell. Just before the date fixed for his execution, the prisoner escaped but was only at liberty a few hours before he was captured and returned to jail. This time added precautions were taken to assure that there would be no further escape to cheat the gallows of its prey.

Many people of the county began to believe that Sheely was innocent of the crime. A fear of grave injustice to this helpless man, doomed to die for the crime of possibly another, resulted in efforts to procure a further respite, but all was in vain.

The dawn of November 19, 1847, witnessed the largest crowd ever to assemble in the little county seat town of Cynthiana. The people came from far and near on horseback, muleback, wagon train and afoot. The excitement of the time is indescribable. Just north of the town is a beautiful wooded bluegrass hill. On this lovely bit of landscape a gallows was erected. A rude coffin was placed on a two-horse wagon and taken to the jail. David walked slowly out of the door of the prison, climbed upon the wagon and sat on his coffin. An escort for this gruesome parade was furnished by the sheriff, his special deputies and the jailer, riding on horseback immediately before and behind the wagon. The entourage moved at a slow pace through the full length of the main street of the town for all to witness the fate of those who take the life of another. Before an assemblage of several hundred people, the condemned man mounted the platform of the scaffold. His feet had touched the soil of his beloved Harrison County for the last time. The hangman's noose was adjusted by the sheriff and placed loosely, but securely, about his neck. In the hazy, shimmering sunlight of that Indian summer morning, David Sheely looked into the faces of many of his former neighbors and friends. The sheriff stepped up beside him and read the order and judgment of the court fixing the method of execution. He tested the rope and saw that the feet of his subject were squarely fixed upon the trap.

"I am directed," said the officer, "to state to you that you have reached the last moments of your life. There is now no further hope of reprieve or pardon. For the last time you are given the opportunity to acknowledge your crime and to pray forgiveness. Are you prepared to make a final statement? Do you have anything to say, David?"

The prisoner looked at the sheriff and again at the crowd. He half raised his arms in an appealing manner, then as if in absolute hopelessness dropped them to his side. Then came the answer in a voice quavering with fear. "If I killed Nancy Sheely, I don't know it. I never had nothin' agin her."

It has been handed down in out county from those who witnessed this spectacle that David's last movement was to turn his head toward the hill country in which he had spent his life. The trap was sprung and a supposed felon was dead.

Aftermath

But this was not the end of David Sheely for the people of Cynthiana and Harrison County. Later events were to establish beyond doubt that he had been convicted and executed for a crime he did not commit. To add to the wrong of taking an innocent life, the physicians of the county in the interest of science subjected his body to dissection and preserved his skeleton for enlightenment of the medical profession; thus compounding the community's mistake by adding the disrespect of disinterring the remains and carving them up. Such treatment of the departed was practiced only upon criminals.

In protest of these wrongs against him, the ghost of David Sheely walked the hills and vales of this county for many years. Notwithstanding the failure to believe in ghosts on the part of the intelligentsia, there is respectable authority that this was one ghost that was different and our county's ghost was the exception that proved the rule!

The *Chronicles of Cynthiana,* by Mrs. Lucinda Boyd, was published in 1894. This delightful and charming book is a collector's item of substantial value. Those fortunate enough to own a copy cannot be tempted to part with it at any price. Mrs. Boyd was a scholarly and well educated woman. She was the daughter of a Christian Church preacher, the wife of a circuit court judge and mother of many children, among them one lawyer, two doctors and a school teacher. I, of course, decline to vouch for the authenticity of our Harrison County ghost, but leave it to Mrs. Boyd who wrote about it in her book at a time much closer to the recorded events.

"Still David Sheely walked the earth an injured, restless, unhappy shade, with a rope around his neck that trailed far behind him on the ground. Many persons in and around Cynthiana *protest that they have seen him.*

"Tradition hath it, that the first time he appeared was on a festive occasion. He left the neighborhood of the hill on which he had suffered death, and haunted a dark ravine above the house now owned by Mrs. Calhoun. In that lonely spot, dense with undergrowth, years and years ago, a murdered man lay dead, and his blood stained the fallen leaves, and crept into the ground, and cried to God for vengeance. But the murderer was never found. This ravine is on the Leesburg pike. Not many miles from Leesburg, in December 1847, was an old farmhouse that had been untenanted for months. The young ladies and gentlemen determined to have a dance in it on Christmas eve. Invitations were issued, and all preparations were made by the young people of the neighborhood for the ball.

"About dark, a little Negro boy was sent to build a wood fire on the wide hearth of the deserted house. He built the fire, and, when it was blazing brightly, he started for home. On his way, he was compelled to pass a grave on the roadside that had been there so long that the oldest inhabitant had no idea who slept beneath the sunken sod. When he came near this lonely grave, David Sheely's ghost arose out of it, white and tall, with the rope thrown over his arm, and his eyes starting out of his head. He looked at the Negro boy, and said: 'There's nobody here but you and me to-night.' The Negro took to his heels, and ran for his life, and fell into his mother's cabin door in a breathless state of excitement. 'What's the matter? You done took leave of your senses, you fool?' said the boy's mother. 'Time I done shook the life out of you; you goin' to talk?' The boy found his breath, and told what he had seen, and was a hero among the Negroes ever afterward.

"Bill, the fiddler, was the first to arrive at the deserted house after the fire was built. He drew a chair near the blazing logs. . . .

"When he was comfortable, he took his beloved fiddle from its case, and warmed and tuned it, and began to play a 'dance tune.' He had not been thus engaged long, when he heard, in a room above him, a man walking, dragging something on the floor that made a sound like a trailing rope. He heard footsteps descend the stairway. When they came to the door, there were three loud raps. Bill said: 'Come in; you're not goin' to scare me with you foolishness.' In it came, with the trailing rope behind it, and said: 'Nobody here but you and me to-night.' Bill sprang to his feet, put his fiddle hurriedly in its case, and cleared the front door at a bound, and took his way home as the crow flies. But David Sheely's ghost pursued him, and he never stopped to scale a fence or jump a ditch that he did not hear, away off, 'Nobody here but you and me to-night.'

"The next thing David's ghost did was terrible.

"There was a young man (who shall be nameless) returning from a visit to his sweetheart. He rode slowly. . . . When he came to the ravine before mentioned, Sheely's ghost jumped on behind him, and began lashing the horse with a rope until it ran away. The young man declared that the arms of the ghost, that sometimes 'hugged him tight,' were as cold as ice, and that he never could have sat his horse if he had not been held on. The horse ran at breakneck speed until it came to the bridge just above Captain Desha's house; there it jumped over the abutment, a distance of ten feet, and broke its neck. The young man was knocked senseless; when he recovered the ghost was gone.

* * *

"That was the last time Sheely's ghost was *seen;* but his bones began to clamor for decent sepulture. When the physician died who owned them, they fell to his daughter, and she put them in her cellar, near to a large furnace that heated her whole house and conservatory.

"One cold night in winter, she invited a young girl to spend the night with her, her husband having gone away on business. It was a bright moonlight night. About midnight, she and the young lady heard the front door bell ring three times. The lady of the house arose at once and looked out of a window that commanded a full view of the front door; but she saw nobody. She discovered that the house was getting cold, and knew that if the fire in the furnace died out she would lose her flowers. She descended the cellar stairs, replenished the fire, and was just opposite Sheely's bones when she heard in her room about the loud report of a pistol. She hurried to her room, expecting to find her dresser on fire; but when she opened the drawer where the pistol lay, there was not a cartridge amiss. It was just as her husband had left it.

"The next day she sent for her minister, and he advised her to bury Sheely's bones.

"She took them in a box and carried them to the hill and near the place where Sheely had suffered death, and gave them decent burial. A few toe bones were lost through a hole in the box while crossing a stream, but Sheely's ghost has never come back in search of them."

Forty years passed. The people of Harrison County, as generations slipped by, gradually forgot the tragedy of Nancy Sheely. Nonetheless, it was revived when a dying man in Maysville, Kentucky, who was said to have been one of the revelers at the Sheely cabin on the night of the murder, called for a notary and made a sworn statement that he, and not Sheely, had killed the woman for reasons he would not reveal.

Many murder cases have been tried in Harrison County since that death bed confession in Maysville. Most of he defendants have been Harrison County citizens and others have been brought here on change of venue from other counties in the state; yet the county's ancient wrong was so deeply impressed upon the minds of its citizens that no jury returned a verdict directing the death sentence for eighty years. Here, Sheely's spirit still takes part in the administration of justice.

Lawyers as jurors

Loquacity of Kentucky lawyers is traditional and can be carried to extremes. The late Ruby Laffoon, Governor of the state from 1932 to 1936 told me of an experience he had as a former circuit judge in one of the courts over which he presided in western Kentucky. He said the court was coming to the end of its trial docket, and but one jury case remained to be tried. The jury in the preceding trial was considering the case in the jury room. For various reasons many jurors had been excused throughout the term. When the case was called for trial and each side had announced ready, it was noted that there were no jurors. The panel had been exhausted. Several members of the bar were in the courtroom for one reason or another, and the then Judge Laffoon, always resourceful, suggested that rather than have the sheriff go out on the street and summon bystanders, the parties might agree to empanel a jury from the lawyers present and thereby save time and expense to the litigants. The plan was acceptable and twelve attorneys took their seats in the jury box.

The case was a very short one but proceeded with due formality, with written instructions from the court, final arguments and all. The jury retired to consider the case. Governor Laffoon said he supposed this jury of lawyers would make short work of the case and report a verdict in a very few minutes. Instead, nothing was heard from the jury for an hour and a half. The judge, anxious to close the term, and with some vexation, directed the sheriff to go to the jury room and ask if the jury was about ready to report.

The sheriff returned from the jury room and explained that he had been told that the jury had not yet taken up the case for consideration. The lawyers were still making nominating speeches for foreman!

Great teacher

Many members of the bar of Kentucky attended the Law School of the University of Virginia. It is said that any lasting, worthwhile institution is but the lengthening shadow of some one man. It might be said of this law school that it is to a large degree the product of the mind, heart, and effort of its revered teacher, John B. Minor. "He taught the law and the reason therefor" at Virginia from 1845 until his death in 1895. For half a century this dedicated scholar and instructor impressed upon the minds of his students the basic fundamentals of the law. Even more than this, he engendered in them an abiding affection, born of respect and admiration, which, after all, is the mark of the truly great leader in any field.

At the close of each school year he delivered a farewell address at the last meeting of the senior class, which he closed with a quotation from Lord Coke: "Wishing unto you the gladsome light of jurisprudence, the loveliness of temperance, the stability of fortitude and the solidity of justice."

One of the Kentucky lawyers who was privileged to sit at the feet of Professor Minor was Mr. Ernest Anderson of Owensboro. Mr. Anderson was a leader of the bar of Kentucky for many years and regarded among his contemporaries as a profound and resourceful lawyer of the highest integrity. He told me this story of his experience as a student at Virginia. He emphasized the high regard which members of the senior class had for Mr. Minor. The graduating class of which he was a member had nine members. They presented to the law school a bust of their beloved teacher. One of the members of the class was a boy who was totally blind but who had made the best scholastic record. On the day of the presentation and unveiling of the bust, a ceremony was held in which each member of the class made fitting remarks and with a sharp instrument cut a small niche in the base on which the bust rested as a final mark of respect. The blind boy was the last to speak and closed with this line: "Thou art unveiled to all save me; yet in my heart there is a niche reserved for thee."

Giant and dwarf

Humorous instances in hearings before appellate courts, while not so numerous as in trial courts, do occur, and without materially impairing the dignity of the court. The following story which was told to me and attributed to the late John Holt of West Virginia may be a stock story, but I have always felt it presented a truly philosophical approach to an apparently hopeless courtroom situation. Since West Virginia is our sister state on the east and many of her fine lawyers practice in the federal courts at Catlettsburg and Pikeville, I will give this account of the resourcefulness of one of the most distinguished members of her bar. I never knew Mr. Holt but have heard of him quite frequently and know of his renown in both his native state and in eastern Kentucky.

It seems that on an occasion he was waiting in the United States Supreme Court Room to present a motion in a very important railroad case. The case immediately preceding his was called and Mr. John W. Davis of New York, recognized pre-eminent leader of the American bar for many years, arose to address the court. Upon Mr. Davis' addressing the court, Mr. Holt was somewhat stunned to learn that the court was being asked for a ruling on the question which he himself was there to present, but gratified to learn that Mr. Davis was urging the court to rule as he proposed to ask. In other words, he and Davis were taking identical positions and seeking identical rulings.

After the distinguished New York lawyer concluded, the court held a brief conference at the bench and, without hearing the attorney for the opposition, overruled Mr. Davis' motion and called for the next case. Mr. Holt arose and stated his motion, but before he could proceed with his argument, Chief Justice Taft leaned forward and with apologies for the interruption asked if counsel had not heard the court's ruling on a similar motion in the past few minutes. Mr. Holt conceded that his motion was identical. The gracious Chief Justice then asked if Holt felt that he could present the question more effectively than John W. Davis. The court stated that it did not want to deny his right to be heard but felt that repetition was only imposing upon the time of the court and unless assurance could be given that Holt felt his argument would be more effective he would be requested to desist. Holt made this classic reply.

"Your Honor, I, of course, cannot compare my knowledge of the law or my ability to present it with that of the gentleman who has just preceded me, but a dwarf sitting on the shoulders of a giant can see farther than the giant."

The good-natured Taft smiled, sat back in his chair and told him to proceed with his argument. The results were the same and "giant" and "dwarf" left to courtroom together, equally unsuccessful.

Naturalization hearings

One of the more pleasant and inspiring duties of my judicial service has been in the conduct of naturalization hearings. It has been my purpose to hold these sessions within reasonable bounds and not yield to a public demand that they be more greatly exploited. I have felt that for a person to forever renounce his fidelity to his native land and swear allegiance to an adopted country calls for something more than the perfunctory taking of an oath. On the other hand, to subject the new-made citizens to pageantry and unwarranted ceremony is to give them a false sense of the true value of American citizenship. Consequently, I have tried to conduct such procedures with scrupulous dignity and impressiveness by having some local patriotic society, where it has volunteered to do so, take part and I conclude with a few remarks from the bench on the obligations as well as the privileges of American citizenship.

Immediately before and throughout the Second World War there were hundreds of petitions for American citizenship. This was due in some measure to requirements of defense plants that all employees be citizens and the natural consequence of calling to the minds of the foreign-born the importance of this step which they had grossly neglected since first being eligible for citizenship.

While our naturalization service is efficient, I had some concern that maybe spies or saboteurs might use this method of getting into our defense plants or on the inside of some military secret project. Throughout the war I was always conscious of a feeling of responsibility for admitting nationals of Germany and Italy with whose countries we were engaged in a life and death struggle for our survival. I was afraid I would read in the paper of some factory for manufacture of vital war materials being blown up and that the accused was someone whom I had admitted to citizenship. Fortunately, my concern was unfounded. We Americans, who have been so blessed with our birthright, are inclined, I am afraid, to be suspicious. I am convinced that there were no more patriotic American citizens than thousands of Germans, Italians, Japanese and other foreign-born persons in our country throughout the second great war. In fact, I am inclined to the belief that many of them appreciate our country and the things for which it stands a great deal more than many of us who have generations of native-born Americans behind us.

Whose America is this?

This fact was brought home to me during the war when I was conducting a naturalization class at a term of court at Pikeville. There were about forty petitioners, the great majority of whom were coal miners and their families. Following our accustomed practice of having the naturalization agent engage each petitioner in a short examination, a woman of about sixty years of age was asked to stand. I shall call her Mrs. Kolinsky from Hungary, the wife of a coal miner who lived in a remote coal camp in Pike County. She was large and ill kept in appearance. She was illiterate and had practically no knowledge of the English language, either to speak it or understand it; and it was with extreme difficulty that the examination progressed. She apparently knew but one name in American history, George Washington. She was asked who was the first President of the United States. She promptly answered, "George Washington." The next question was, "Who is the present President of the United States?" She answered, "George Washington."

After some prompting by the examiner, she mumbled what, in charity, might be accepted as the name Roosevelt. The next questions were put to her as simply as possible but she evidenced absolutely no understanding. I began to wonder whether she was a fit subject for admission and was on the verge of telling her to stand aside with an admonition to the agent that such persons should not be presented for citizenship. But the agent knew much more of the quality of this fine person than her appearance and halting speech revealed. His next question was, "Mrs. Kolinsky, how many children do you have?"

Her swarthy face brightened into a broad smile at the sound of the word "children." She promptly answered, "Nine."

"How many boys?"

"Six."

"Where is John?" he asked

Almost eagerly, she replied, "On Bataan with McArter."

"Where is Joe?"

"Joe he with Gen'l Patton."

"What about Ken?" (I learned later that Ken was short for Kentucky.)

"On ocean—battleship," was her quick response.

"Where is Ollie?"

With this question the smile left her face. She shook her head and wiped her eyes with her apron. The agent sensed the situation and hurried on to the next question.

"What about little Gus?"

The smile of pride returned to her face and she replied, "Fort Knox, next week."

The one other son was a polio victim which accounted for his failure to volunteer for military service. As to Ollie, I learned that he was overseas and had been reported missing in action.

With real pride she took her oath of citizenship and I wondered whether there was anyone in the room who was more entitled to that honor.

* * *

Another interesting experience in naturalization comes to mind. On an occasion at Covington we had for admission a class of sixty persons. Among them was a man of about seventy-six years of age. He was exceptionally well-dressed and very intelligent looking. I learned that he was a successful businessman of Cincinnati and a subject of Great Britain.

When the naturalization examiner asked him his place of birth, he answered Scotland. He was then asked, "How long have you lived in the United States?"

He replied, "Seventy-six years."

The examiner said, "Have you always thought you were a citizen of this country?"

He answered, "Yes, and still think so."

He took the oath with the others and court recessed. I was interested in finding out about this man and the reason for his answers. The naturalization agent gave me this account.

His father and mother were natives of Scotland and from very old and respected families in the Highlands. They had married in Scotland and had come immediately to America. When it was learned that a baby was to be born, the father began to save his money for the purpose of a return trip to his native Scotland. He had been born on an ancestral estate which had been the birthplace of his lineal forebears for four hundred years and he wanted his child to be born there, too. When the time of the expected birth was about to arrive, he put the mother on a boat bound for England with a round trip ticket. She returned to Scotland. The baby (our petitioner) was born and in two weeks was brought back to America.

No striped pants

Colonel William Colston of the Cincinnati law firm of Harmon, Colston, Goldsmith and Hoadly, was a well known attorney in Kentucky. He was a Confederate veteran and, I am told, lost an arm in the service of the Southern cause. He was counsel for the Southern Railway System for many years. At one time when he had a case to argue before the United States Supreme Court, he took the president of the company to Washington with him. While they were waiting for their case to be heard, the client wandered about the building, inquiring of the habits and practices of the justices in the conduct of the business of the court. He found a bailiff who was glad to answer all questions and who entertained him with various stories of incidents in connection with sessions of that eminent tribunal. One thing he learned was that there was a rule of court that any attorney addressing it must wear a vest. "You see," the garrulous attache elaborated, "some of the attorneys go far beyond the rules and appeal to the vanity of the judges by dressing in formal attire, with striped trousers and cutaway coat. Your lawyer is complying with the rules by wearing a vest but has on only a plain business suit."

Several weeks later the ruling of the court came down deciding the case against the railroad. Colonel Colston immediately phoned the company and talked to the gentleman who had been with him in Washington. "Well, we lost our case," he said. "I know why," was the disgruntled response. "Why?" asked the Colonel. "Because you weren't dressed right," said the president. To which came the rejoinder from the disappointed but still belligerent Colonel Colston, "Well, by God, that's a better reason than any they gave in the opinion."

Rules of court

Speaking of rules of court, it has always been my belief that the fewer rules a court has the less difficulty it has in dispatching business. This applies particularly to local rules. It is the purpose of both the Civil and Criminal Rules of Federal Procedure to make the practice throughout the country uniform so that lawyers from distant places will not be hampered with local requirements entirely foreign to their accustomed practice. I heard Judge Cochran say that the only time he knew he had a rule was when someone cited his own rule to him to keep him from doing what he should do to further the progress of the litigation.

Trial judges are beset by many difficulties and if care is not taken they can easily fall into either dictatorial or slovenly informal practices which may cause the court to lose certain respect of the bar and public. The high office of a judge should be above reproach.

Obligations of the judiciary

Sir Francis Bacon said of judges, "They should imitate God in whose seat they sit." I was discussing this statement with a judge friend of mine one time. He remarked that that was impossible, which, of course, it is; but I suggested that maybe we could be more like God than we are or at least we might strengthen our characters in that direction by our awareness of the statement of one scholar and thinker.

The idealism of our judicial calling, with special emphasis on the trial judge, is eloquently expressed in the following words of Josiah Quincy:

"The more vicious, the more base, the more abandoned the class of society, on which any department of justice acts, the more and the weightier is the reason, that those who administer it should be elevated above all interest, and all fear, and all suspicion, and all reproach. Everywhere the robe of justice should be spotless; but in that part, where it is destined to touch the ground, where from its use, it must mix with the soil, there its texture should contain and preserve whatever there is of celestial quality in human life and conduct, there, if possible, its ermine should dazzle, by exceeding whiteness; and be steeped, not only with the deep fountains of human learning, but be purified in those heavenly dews which descend alone from the source of divine and eternal justice."

I have been on the bench many years and have, I hope, gained some impressions of the intellectual and moral obligations of those who serve as presiding judges in the trial of both criminal and civil cases.

In the first place, I believe one who assumes the judicial office should abjure all ambition to hold other political office. I do not think further preferment should be denied by law but solely by the individual's own dedication to judicial service. I have always felt that Charles Evans Hughes, great statesman, scholar and judge that he was, lowered the dignity of a justice of the Supreme Court when he permitted himself to be nominated for the presidency. A judge should want to be nothing other than a judge.

To all citizens the court is a permanent structure and a part of the bedrock of their government. When a judge tries a case he himself is on trial. Thus it behooves him who presides in the *nisi prius* court to be ever conscious of the fact that the fairness, integrity, greatness, and justice of his country may be judged by his own fairness, integrity, greatness and justice. He should respect the bench upon which he sits and the courtroom in which he presides as a sanctuary wherein all else is put aside so that equal and exact justice may be done.

The atmosphere of the courtroom should not be too formal or stiff; but there should be a quiet dignity and there should be, to borrow a phrase from one of my brothers of the bench in describing the court in which a certain judge presided, "a sort of homey feeling," that even the most lowly defendant before the bar, the young and inexperienced attorney, or the casual observer, may have a feeling of ease.

The judge should begin court promptly after each adjournment and should dispatch the business of the session as quickly and economically as possible. However, it should not be overlooked that the court is not privileged to exist because it is swift or because it is cheap. And no whit of the orderly procedure of dispensing justice should be sacrificed to such imposters.

Court should be formal and all hearings, motions and trials held in the courtroom. I am strongly opposed to anything giving the impression of star chamber. We as lawyers and judges must be ever mindful of the fact that lay people view with suspicion all proceedings behind closed doors. When the judge and the lawyers withdraw from the litigants and the public to the judge's chambers, they subject themselves to criticism.

I believe courts in recent times have lost some of their color. The federal courts especially are so jealous of their dignity that they and many of the state courts have about bluffed lawyers out of making good speeches by throwing in a few stories or quoting from the Scriptures or classical literature as in the so-called "old days."

Personally, I do not feel that an attorney should be too severely restrained. Christ taught by parables, and an appropriate story to illustrate a point might be just the thing to further the cause of justice. Consequently, I am rather lenient and somewhat encourage lawyers to feel free to express themselves in closing arguments in what they believe to be the most effective way to present their client's case.

I enjoy hearing a good speech but, of course, take all precautions to see that there is no departure of any significance from the record.

Umbrellas

One of the most interesting and entertaining lawyers I have known is Mr. Abraham Berkowitz of the Birmingham, Alabama bar. He was before me in the trial of a case in Louisville, and in his closing argument told one of the most humorous stories, by way of illustration, I have heard. He was impressing the jury with the fact that it was so easy to be misunderstood and that many times evidence of obvious facts was entirely foreign to the actual facts of the situation.

He said some years ago when he was about to leave home for his office it began to rain. This reminded his wife of the fact that two of their umbrellas were in need of repair. Just before he left the house to catch his bus, his mother-in-law phoned and asked him to stop by her home and pick up a couple of umbrellas and take them to the repairman for her. This he did and before reaching his office, stopped at the repair shop and left the umbrellas. At noon he had lunch at a restaurant just across the street. When he had finished he took his hat and coat and picked up an umbrella hanging on the rack. As he was about to leave, a young lady stopped him and said, "You have my umbrella." Mr. Berkowitz apologized profusely and offered excuses for his careless mistake. The young lady took her umbrella but without much show of acceptance of his explanation.

When Berkowitz left his office in the afternoon, he stopped by the shop, picked up the four repaired umbrellas and caught a bus home. After he was seated he looked across the aisle and who should he see but the young lady of the restaurant incident, who was gazing at him and his four umbrellas with a look of utter contempt. Abe is a friendly and affable man, and while feeling very much embarrassed, he said he nodded and smiled but received in return only a cold stare and a turning away of the head. A few blocks farther on the bus stopped and the young lady arose to leave. As she stepped past his seat, she stopped momentarily and gazing at him in scorn said, "Well, you've had a good day, haven't you?" The illustration went over well with the jury and no whit of the dignity of the court was lost.

Solid foundation

Orie S. Ware of Covington is a lawyer of ability and an excellent storyteller. He gives the following story which, to my mind, is one of the real gems of Kentucky courthouse lore.

It seems that the owner of a large Covington office building near the banks of the Ohio River sold it to an investor. The building sat on a fill of new made ground and, according to best engineering practices, required a foundation of particular specifications in quantity of steel and cement. The seller had, according to the complainant, warranted the building as having the necessary underpinning. Shortly after the transfer the new owner saw that the building gave evidence of sinking. Cracks came in the walls and it appeared that his investment was about to be lost.

Through his attorney, Mr. Ware, he sued the grantor for a rescission of the contract and damages for breach of warranty. The defendants denied the allegations of the petition (complaint) and plead by way of confession and avoidance that even though the foundation might not contain all the ingredients he had represented it to, it was nevertheless a good foundation and entirely adequate for the kind and size of building it supported.

Mr. Omer Rogers, an eminent lawyer of Boone County and Covington, represented the defendant. The issues were made, and the trial date having arrived, a jury was selected and the litigants and their capable counsel repaired to the battle.

As an important feature of this episode, it must be pointed out that the circuit courtroom in Covington at that time had a very large and beautiful clock hanging on the wall opposite the judge's bench. While not unlike in appearance the old Victorian clocks in public buildings of a former era, this one was singularly different in one important particular. It struck on the hour and the half hour and when it was striking, with its melodious but loud gong, all proceedings in the court had to stand still until the striking was concluded.

The plaintiff testified and introduced other witnesses showing the nature of the damage to the building and the kind of foundation under it. He did a thing which is sometimes dangerous, but if it works is the most effective strategy in the trial of a lawsuit. He saved his best witness to be used in rebuttal.

The plaintiff closed and the defendant offered his proof. In his own testimony he denied the damage to the building and offered proof by two local contractors who testified that in their opinion the formula used in mixing the concrete for the foundation was entirely adequate.

In rebuttal, the plaintiff called his star witness, a Colonel Johnson, formerly of the United States Army Engineers and presently consulting engineer for one of the largest building contractors of Cincinnati. The witness qualified as an expert, giving his educational background and practical experience. He was a very tall and handsome individual about seventy years of age with an erect military bearing. His testimony was most effective and was obviously producing telling results. The jury was impressed by his manner and the substance of what he was saying to them.

When the direct examination was concluded, the witness was passed to defense counsel for cross-examination.

Mr. Rogers was a trial lawyer of no mean ability. He was square of frame and jaw and when aroused gave the appearance of a pit-bull terrier pawing to get at his prey. This witness had without doubt excited him. He knew his case was to be won or lost depending upon the effectiveness of failure of his cross-examination. He settled down to what he hoped would be a successful battle of wits with a clever witness. With set jaw and fire in his eye, Mr. Rogers sailed in.

"Mr. Johnson—I believe you said that was your name, didn't you?" he asked.

"Yes, sir," was the calm reply.

"You said you were a retired Army officer and a graduate engineer, I believe?"

"Yes, sir."

"You say you graduated from Purdue University and Massachusetts Institute of Technology?"

"Yes, sir."

"You are now the chief consulting engineer of a large Cincinnati building company?"

"Yes, sir."

"You were on the staff of General William L. Sibert in constructing roads for military purposes in France during the World War, were you not?"

"Yes, sir."

"You were one of the principal consulting engineers in the planning of the Carew Tower and other large buildings in Cincinnati, I believe?"

"Yes, sir."

"You have heard these reputable Covington contractors testify that this foundation was adequate, haven't you?"

"Yes, sir."

Then came the big question. Rogers leaned forward in his chair, his steel blue eyes spitting fire and with something of a sarcastic snarl in his speech stated, "Now, Colonel Johnson, with all your high-flown attempted show of knowledge, I want you to tell this jury what *you* think is the best foundation."

The witness drew himself up on his chair and gazed steadily at his questioner. "Mr. Rogers," he said, "in answer to your question, I refer you to the Gospel according to Saint Matthew, the Seventh Chapter and twenty-fourth verse, wherein it is recorded that the wise man built his house upon a rock, and the rain descended, and the floods came, and the winds blew, and beat upon that house and it fell not: for it was founded upon a rock. And the foolish man built his house upon the sand: and the rain descended, and the floods came, and the winds blew, and beat upon that house and it fell for it was built upon the sands."

So impressive was the compelling voice of the striking figure in the witness box, uttering these truths from Holy Writ that even the tenacious cross-examiner was momentarily stunned. The courtroom held a death-like silence. Before the spell was broken, the hands of the old clock had simultaneously reached the hour of high noon and she began to boom out her twelve strokes. Everyone sat waiting. When the striking was ended, Judge Rodney Bryson turned to the sheriff and said, "Mr. Sheriff, you may announce a recess of the court until 1:00 P.M."

The jury retired and the audience left the courtroom. Mr. Rogers got up from his chair, knowing that he was badly beaten, and walked over to Mr. Ware. He leaned over and whispered, "Orie, when that old bird finished that damned sermon, instead of Bryson saying 'Mr. Sheriff, you may recess court,' he should have said, 'We will all now rise and receive the benediction.'"

Old-fashioned orator

All Kentuckians who knew him personally and who had intimate association with him had a genuine affection for the late Governor Edwin P. Morrow of Somerset. He was a man of warm and friendly disposition, a gifted orator, and a very resourceful lawyer when occasion demanded.

I recall quite well the last time I saw him. It was in the federal courtroom in Lexington where he was defending an elderly doctor charged with violation of the narcotic law. I, as United States Attorney, was putting forth every effort to get a conviction of what I sincerely felt was a serious law violation. Ed Morrow, with equal conviction of his client's innocence, was determined that there should be an acquittal.

President Theodore Roosevelt said that an aggressive fight for right is the noblest sport known to man. With both of us assured we were fighting for the right, you may well understand what a day of noble sport this trial was. About four o'clock in the afternoon it was obvious that the case could not be concluded that day and would likely take all of the next. Mr. Morrow came to me and said, "You've got me in a bad fix. When I accepted this employment, I was assured and believed the trial could be concluded in one day. Now it appears we cannot possibly finish today and may not be able to tomorrow. I accepted an invitation to deliver the keynote speech at the Republican state convention out here at Woodland Auditorium and unless you will help me out, I'll have to cancel my speech. Would you be willing to consent to a mistrial and take the case up at a later date? If not, I must stay with my client, but will have to forego the delight of giving you Democrats hell out here at the Auditorium for a full hour and a half tomorrow afternoon."

I assured him that I was convinced that giving us Democrats hell was about all the Republicans were going to get out of the election and I wasn't going to stand in the way of what little fun they were going to have. With that we both went to Judge Church Ford who was presiding and on Ed's motion and without objection the swearing of the jury was set aside and the case reassigned for trial.

He made his speech on the next day as planned and although I didn't hear it, I know it was a good one. He was stricken in his last illness that afternoon on the bus on his way to Frankfort and died very shortly thereafter.

I always appreciated his friendship and the privilege of rendering him an accommodation in his last courthouse appearance.

* * *

Senator John Sherman Cooper tells this story about Ed Morrow when he was a practicing lawyer in Somerset. A man went into Morrow's office late one afternoon and asked him to help him in his trial to following morning at nine o'clock. Ed said, "Well, this is short notice, but what are you charged with?"

"Wilful murder," was the reply.

"Man, do you mean to tell me you are going on trial for murder in the morning and are just now getting you a lawyer?"

"Oh, no," said the prospective client, "I've got my lawyer, Judge Bethurum, he'll try the case; but Ed, I want you to come over and sympathize with the jury."

"Old Ring"

Notwithstanding his many courthouse battles and his wide law practice for a generation throughout Kentucky, Governor Morrow is probably best remembered for his famous "Old Ring" speech delivered in practically every courthouse in Kentucky from the Big Sandy at the West Virginia border to Mills Point on the Mississippi in his race for governor against James D. Black, the Democratic nominee, in 1919.

Back in those days, there wasn't much issue between the Democratic and Republican parties in local Kentucky politics. The Democratic party was dominant, of course, and when united was unbeatable; but it had been split asunder for several years by the factionalism of the Owsley Stanley and J. C. W. Beckham followers. Governor Stanley had beaten Morrow for governor by only four hundred votes four years before. The time was ripe for a Republican to win if he could find an issue and had the personality and forensic ability to exploit it. Ed Morrow had the ability and he dug up an issue that literally drove the electorate mad with enthusiasm.

A Kentuckian equally, if not to a much greater extent than other Americans, loves his dog. Next to his wife and children the thing closest to his heart is this humble and faithful four footed companion. It is traditional in our state that when the early pioneer came through Cumberland Gap, he carried with him an axe and a Bible, while trotting behind his covered wagon or at his heels was a hound dog. No other race of men take more literally to heart the following words from Senator Vest's immortal speech:

> "The one absolutely unselfish friend that man can have in this selfish world, the one that never deserts him, the one that never proves ungrateful or treacherous, is his dog. A man's dog stands by him in prosperity and in poverty, in health and in sickness. He will sleep on the cold ground, where the wintry winds blow and the snow drives fiercely, if only he may be near his master's side. He will kiss the hand that has no food to offer; he will lick the wounds and sores that come in encounters with the roughness of the world. He guards the sleep of his pauper master as if he were a prince. When all other friends desert, he remains. When riches take wings and reputation falls to pieces, he is as constant in his love as the sun in its journey through the heavens."

Master psychologist that he was and with an infinite knowledge of the emotions of his fellow Kentuckians, Ed

Morrow selected as his issue the repeal of the state law requiring an owner to buy a license for his dog or see the dog impounded by the sheriff and destroyed. Not only was the owner to buy a license but he must impose upon his staunch ally and guardian the onerous burden of wearing a license tag attached to a collar around his neck. To anticipate momentarily the conclusion of this story, when Ed concluded his campaign speaking tour, a collar was the symbol of canine humiliation and embarrassment.

His speeches on the repeal of the "Dog Law" are classics in Kentucky political lore. Noted speaker and entertainer that he was, he always attracted a crowd at the county courthouses where he was scheduled to speak in behalf of his candidacy for the office of governor. Some may think that such an issue would appeal to only rural Kentucky, but that proved not true. The speech was received with equal relish in urban communities. It was, however, more adapted to the small town crowds.

After getting his audience relaxed by a few entertaining stories and the usual attack on the opposition for "extravagance and waste of the taxpayer's hard earned money," he would conclude his speech on the main theme: a promise, if elected governor, to take up as the first order of business the outright repeal of "the most cruel and unjust law that had ever been enacted." He would throw his magnetic personality and his compelling voice at his sympathetic audiences with a zeal that held them spellbound.

"When you farmers go home tonight," he would say, "who will be at the gate to meet you? The one faithful ally who has been standing there all day awaiting patiently your return from town. With a whine or soft bark of sincere joy he will bound to meet you and grab your hand lovingly and playfully in his mouth. He will stand behind you as you unsaddle your mule or unhitch your horse from the spring-wagon or buggy; he will trot at your heels as you do your night work; he will stand near you as you sit on that stool and milk your cow. After you have had the supper which your good wife has prepared, you will find that easy chair in front of the open fire. As you sit there dozing you will hear a scratching at the kitchen door. You will go there and let him in and the shaggy form will stretch out in front of the fire at your feet or beside your chair. At the slightest move of the chair you will hear the thump, thump of his tail upon the floor to remind you that in all the world there in no constancy to compare with his. He will raise his dark brown eyes to gaze at his idol. Your hand will reach for that devoted head and a soft muzzle will be gently thrust into it. As you stroke that head and neck, your hand will come in contact with a hard and unyielding object, the tag collar. It is then I want you to recall my words and say to him, 'Ring, it won't be long until you will again be free. I was in town today and Ed Morrow made a speech and told us when he goes to Frankfort as our new governor, he is going to take away your shame and restore you to your rights as a true Kentuckian. Ed knows how you have suffered and is going to set you free.'"

This peroration drew wild applause. Morrow was elected, the bill to repeal the dog tax law was introduced in the Legislature as an administration measure and twice defeated. I do not doubt the sincerity of the governor, but now, after more than four decades, old Ring is still collared.

Sho' 'nuf bad weather

One of the best storytellers I have ever known is U.S. District Judge Leslie Darr of the Eastern District of Tennessee, Chattanooga Division. Before going on the federal bench, Judge Darr was a state circuit judge and relates many instances that occurred while serving in that office.

On an occasion of severe winter weather, the court was engaged in the trial of a lawsuit in which a leading doctor in the rural town where court was sitting was a main witness. The inclement weather had produced widespread sickness and because of an almost overwhelming schedule of calls on his patients, the doctor requested the court to permit him to remain in his office until time for him to testify. His office was just across the street from the courthouse and as he was in easy access, the request was granted as an accommodation, not only to the doctor but to the community. When it came time for the doctor's testimony, court took a short recess while the sheriff went to the doctor's office to summon him. The extreme cold weather had penetrated the courtroom and while waiting for the witness, the judge, litigants and jurors huddled around the large pot-bellied cast iron stove which was the only source of heat in the building.

In a few minutes the sheriff returned and announced to the judge that the girl in the doctor's office told him that the doctor had been called from his office on an emergency obstetrics case. Judge Darr said that was too bad, but court would just have to wait for awhile. Turning to the sheriff, he said, "Did you say it was a case of obstetrics?"

"That's what the lady said," replied the sheriff, "and I'll tell you, Judge, if this weather don't let up, we'll all have it."

Henry Clay

The stories of the exploits at the bar of Kentucky's distinguished forensic giant, Henry Clay, are myriad, but I heard one many years ago which I cannot recall having ever seen in print. At least I am confident many of the younger generations of lawyers have not heard it. It was told by one of our state's most illustrious and brilliant lawyers, Thomas F. Marshall of Lexington and Woodford County.

Marshall was much younger than Clay and when he came to the bar, Clay, then a member of Congress, was regarded as the outstanding trial lawyer of Kentucky. Marshall, very unfortunately, came to an early grave, due largely, it is said, to his dissipation. His success was marred by profligate habits, and his potential capabilities were never realized. His partner was another eminent Lexingtonian, Robert J. Breckinridge. Mr. Breckinridge, after a few years at the bar, abandoned the law and went into the Presbyterian ministry.

As young lawyers, Breckinridge and Marshall knew that if they could get a case in which Clay was their opponent and be successful in winning it, their reputations were established. Fortune was on their side and they were employed in a case to contest a will in which Clay was representing the estate. When the day of trial arrived, Marshall said the enthusiasm of the young partners knew no bounds. Their preparation, although long and tedious, had been exhaustive. Their presentation was flawless as compared with what he says was a "shabby" display by the opposition. However, the final victory would obviously go to the side that would present the most eloquent arguments to the jury.

Breckinridge opened the closing speeches and presented a masterly oration. Clay's partner was weak. Then Marshall delivered his forceful and telling address which he felt would be unanswerable. "But," he concluded, "when Clay stood before the jury as a master of debate, he raised his hand and with one sweep of that mighty arm sent Breckinridge to the pulpit and me to the gutter."

* * *

On one occasion when Marshall had indulged too freely, he fell in the gutter on his way home. It was the autumn season of the year and the leaves falling from the trees had begun to cover his body. Friends found him there flat on his back almost completely hidden by the blanket of leaves. They looked down upon his prostrate form and one of them remarked, "what a pity to find this brilliant young man lying prone in the street, his manly form covered by the falling autumn leaves."

Marshall opened his eyes. "Leaves," he said, "have their time to fall. So do I. Each from the same cause, getting dry! But the difference between these leaves and me—I fall harder and more frequently."

Look to the hills

The instances of the drama and romance of the bar of Kentucky are confined to no section or part. All have their local and colloquial tales and accounts of the prowess, humor and skill of their orators and lawyers.

One section, however, may have been somewhat neglected in the matter of record and exploitation because of lack of roads and the usual means of communication and intercourse with the rest of Kentucky. I refer to that charming, historical and vast territory known as the mountains. For this part of our state and her attractive and intelligent people I have a deep and abiding affection. No more fitting tribute could be paid than that which is set forth in excerpts from the following address presented at the meeting of the Kentucky State Bar Association at Frankfort in 1933 by a distinguished eastern Kentucky lawyer and, at that time, Attorney General of the Commonwealth, the late Honorable Bailey P. Wooten.

To attempt to paraphrase his remarks would endanger its historical value and detract from its eloquence.

"Let us go back some thirty odd years to a time near the close of the last century and the beginning of the present, to a remote part of the Commonwealth, where highways and railroads were unknown and the beauty of the hills had not been desecrated by their heedless touch; where bridle paths up creeks and over mountains, down rivers and trails lead you through sparsely settled country from one county seat to another; where laurel and rhododendron bloom in spring, and golden leaves glimmer in autumn sun; where the hush of silence is broken only by chattering birds and barking squirrels; and where friendships are measured in terms of life or death.

"In December, 1897, when Judge W. F. Hall closed his last court at the expiration of his term of office as Circuit Judge of the old 26th District at Hazard, Kentucky, there was not a foot of railroad nor a mile of improved dirt road in all that vast territory embraced by Harlan, Leslie, Clay, Owsley, Perry, Knott, Letcher, Pike, Floyd, Magoffin and Jackson Counties, a territory of 150 miles across from railroad to railroad. It embraced the headwaters of the Big Sandy, the Cumberland and the three forks of the Kentucky River. The largest county seat within it had fewer than five hundred people.

"The lawyers attending the courts within this territory at that time travelled the circuit on horseback, as those in the days of Ben Hardin, John Rowan, and others less renowned, had travelled before railroads and modern highways were ever thought of, and when horseback travel from court to court was the only means of conveyance.

"In that day, and until the last of this great wilderness was penetrated by railroads up the Big Sandy in 1899, the Cumberland in 1908, and the Kentucky in 1912, which marked the passing of the circuit riders, the last of their tribe in America, there travelled through this wilderness

such men as Walter Harkins, Jim Marrs, King
Cook, Logan Salyers, Jim Fitzpatrick, Crit Bach,
Ed Hogg, Dan Fields and others who regularly
rode the circuits embraced by these counties.
They were joined at intervals, attention to their
private feuds permitting, by Jim Marcum, Boone
Logan and Fult French.

"The time of this story is the early part of
the present century; the place may be anywhere
within this great circuit; the scene a court house;
time three o'clock P.M. Darkness comes early in
the mountains in these December days. The
jury is dismissed, the sheriff adjourns court until
court in course. The gavel falls, and the judge,
Commonwealth's attorney, and visiting lawyers
are in a commotion to get started to the next
place of holding court, anxious to cover a part
of the forty or fifty miles before pitch dark, that
the rest of the journey may be more easily nego-
tiated on the next day, Sunday following. Pranc-
ing, pawing horses, eager to be gone, and frisking
from a week or ten days' stay in the stable, are
brought up before boarding houses and hotels
in the little county seat; leggings and spurs are
donned, saddlebags are adjusted; an easy swing
into the saddle, a wave of good-bye to the friends
and hosts waiting to see the start, and the judge,
accompanied by his Commonwealth's attorney
and the visiting lawyers, riders of the circuit, are
off. Three or four hours of hard riding brings the
cavalcade to what might be a half dozen regu-

lar stopping places; Jim Hays', on Long Fork of
Buckhorn; Smokey Allen or Anse Hays' on Trou-
blesome; John Spencer or Lige Duff's on Grape-
vine; Jim Lewis' on Coon of Cutskin, but most
likely to Pud Breeding or Spencer Combs' on
Carrs Fork. It is dark, cold and raining, a cheer-
ful firelight can be seen. 'Hello,' comes from one
of the crowd, answered by a rush of the prospective host, the barking of half a dozen dogs, and
a cordial 'Get down and come in,' for the court
and his retinue of lawyers were genuinely welcomed on these three-times-a-year trips. Each
rider, with the possible exception of the judge,
looks after the care of his own horse, for the hard
riders of the hills keep the best blooded horses
the Blue Grass affords in the pink of condition,
for they, as their masters, must have stamina to
withstand the hardships of forced marches over
the mountain trails. Saddle bags and slickers, leggings and spurs are piled in one corner of the
room, about which the firelight throws a soft
glow, and all join in answering a stream of questions from the host who has not, perhaps, had
an opportunity for the news in a month. The
squawk of chickens and the rattle of dishes whet
the appetites, if any whetting is needed, and
warn us of approaching supper. The host pro-
duces from somewhere a something white and
clear from a brown jug, with cornshuck stopper,
and having the kick of a mule. Keen appetites are
soon appeased by fried chicken, cornbread and

hot coffee. During the meal discussions range from law to theology; from 'Who wrote Shakespeare?', to the price of poplar trees. The most intricate points of the law and procedure were regularly and sometimes hotly debated. These were veritable law schools, and those entering into discussion showed a knowledge of the law as laid down by Coke & Blackstone, Greenleaf and Chitty that might well be emulated by the law student of today. References by these lawyers to sections of the Code, Statutes and leading texts were regarded by one another as commonplace. They arrived at their conclusions by process of reasoning, by sound logic, and by knowledge of fundamental principles of justice, and not from a line of cases. These were not case lawyers. The doctrine of *stare decisis* had no lodgment in their minds, for there was not, at that time, a complete set of even the Kentucky Reports within the vast territory mentioned; but if one cared to examine the contents of the saddlebags in the corner of the room, he would most likely find a volume of Blackstone of Greenleaf, or the latest works on land titles and criminal law. He was sure to find Montesquieu's 'Spirit of Laws.'

"Bedtime comes early in the mountains, but a few drinks have set Captain James B. Fitzpatrick, a gallant Confederate soldier, to reciting 'Tam O'Shanter' and 'Twa Dogs.' The more drinks he gets the more dramatic he becomes, and more real the ghost at the Kirk. He carried a dog-eared copy of Bobby Burns in his pocket and knew by heart every poem in it from 'Cotter's Saturday Night' to his favorite, 'The Deil Awa' with the Exciseman.' He probably had in mind 'Revenuers.' Sleep came often to his droning of 'Annie Laurie,' or the 'Lass that made the bed to me.' Morning came all too soon, the time to get up being announced by the vigorous ringing of a farm bell fastened to the end of a pole. A bounteous breakfast is eaten in comparative silence, the convivial spirits of some of the party the night before having become somewhat dampened, giving Crit Bach a chance for a dissertation on the relative merits of Solomon's Proverbs and Paul's Epistles, while Ed Hogg, a Shakespearean scholar of no mean ability, regales the court and host at the other end of the table with good advice from 'Hamlet,' and, with twinkling glance toward the hostess, 'The Taming of the Shrew,' a play he sincerely enjoyed.

"Again the call for horses; a smiling, glad-hearted host, entreating an early return, and all ride out into the mist of early dawn, clattering down the creek bed over stones and through mush ice, a happy throng. Early dusk brings us to the next county seat, where the concourse is met with glad 'how-de-dos' from the populace, all of whom, it seems, have turned out to see the arrival of the court, and to extend to him and the circuit riders a royal welcome.

"Monday morning the court room is packed, hitching space along the horse racks, erected on three sides of the court house, is at a premium, for every able-bodied man in the county came to the opening of the circuit court in those days. The assemblage in the court house is tense as the judge opens his court, empanels his juries and instructs the Grand Jury. These instructions were eagerly listened to by the people, and was an event in their lives and in their conversation thereafter. Many of them were profoundly eloquent, filled with sound advice, and were of lasting good. There was decorum in the court room. The jailor and the high sheriff stood at attention with '45's for ready reference, and, if a feud trial or hotly contested election case was on, they searched each person who entered the door for deadly weapons; but they experienced their greatest difficulty, as a rule, in keeping the laity from monopolizing the space reserved for lawyers.

"Time forbids a recital of all, or even a small part, of the stirring events of those stirring times.

"These men pioneered in the field of law in that section of the State, just as their forefathers had pioneered in the same wilderness, cut off from the outside world, not so many years before.

"But these circuit riding lawyers are no more. They have topped the mountain on their last ride. We see them pause at the top, turn in their saddles, and beckon their fellows—then pass out of sight forever."

The ever-growing law

This effort to briefly record something of the color and romance of the bar of Kentucky as observed these many years must of course be incomplete. The law itself, with its complex, many sidedness, makes a full history of these years impossible. A student of the law is constantly confronted with its paradoxical nature. Solid and fluid, broad and narrow, kind and harsh, changeless and yet ever changing; but as we here in America have learned, it is always eminently fair and impartial. The statue of the blind goddess with evenly balanced scales is no myth but an ever present reality in the cause of justice. One thing the true student or practitioner knows is that the law is not static. It must recognize change.

> "New times demand new measures and new men,
> The old advances and in time outgrows the laws
> Which in our fathers' day were best.
> And after us some purer scheme will be shaped out
> By wiser men than we,
> Made wiser by the steady growth of truth."

At a time of one of the vacancies on the United States Supreme Court during the administration of Woodrow Wilson, a Kentucky delegation from the Congress called on the President to urge the appointment to the court of Circuit Judge J. M. Benton of Winchester. Senator Alben W. Barkley, who told me this story, said Mr. Wilson listened attentively to the chairman of the delegation as he stated the qualifications and virtues of their candidate. At the conclusion of the remarks, Senator Barkley said the

President asked this very significant question, "Gentle-men," he said, "does your candidate believe that the law grows?"

Mr. Wilson, who was probably the most profound scholar of constitutional government and law ever to occupy the office of President, then explained. "The law is not something small but it is something big. It may be likened to a great oak whose ancient beginning is unknown to all living people. For many decades it has stood in the forest and grown into a gigantic tree, giving beauty and shelter to all its surroundings. So long as it grows it will flourish and be of greater beauty and blessing but if there should be placed an iron casement about its trunk it would cease to grow and surely die. The same may be said of the law. It must continue to grow and to reach out and shelter more and more people. Its blessings and security cannot be limited to the fortunate or the few. It must cast its shadow of certain justice over mankind. It must stand for the dignity of the individual throughout all the earth."

The committee, or course, assured the President that Judge Benton met this test and was an advocate of like principles. However, nothing came of the interview. I believe it was at this time that the late Justice Louis D. Brandeis was appointed to the court.

Conclusion

I have given only a glimpse of the Kentucky Lawyer. His is a way of life, an ideal of service, a contribution in the best sense.

> "Be noble, and the nobleness that lies
> In other men, sleeping but never dead
> Will rise, in majesty, to meet thine own."
> —Lowell.

* * * * * * * * *